YOU'RE COOKIN' IT

★ COUNTRY ★

MY FAVORITE RECIPES AND MEMORIES

Loretta Lynn

YOU'RE COOKIN' IT
★ COUNTRY ★
MY FAVORITE RECIPES AND MEMORIES

RUTLEDGE HILL PRESS
A Division of Thomas Nelson Publishers
Since 1798

www.thomasnelson.com

Published by Rutledge Hill Press, a Division of Thomas Nelson, Inc.,
P.O. Box 141000, Nashville, Tennessee, 37214.

Library of Congress Cataloging-in-Publication Data

Lynn, Loretta.
You're cookin' it country : my favorite recipes and memories / by Loretta Lynn.
p. cm.
Includes bibliographical references and index.
ISBN: 1-4016-0179-0 (hardcover)
1. Cookery, American. I. Title.
TX715.L967 2004
641.5973—dc22

2004009266

Printed in the United States of America

04 05 06 07 08 — 9 8 7 6 5 4 3 2 1

*This cookbook is dedicated to my family,
friends, and fans with all my love.*

★CONTENTS★

★ PREFACE ★

My daughter Patsy came home the other day and said, "Mommy, you're going to have to do something about your cooking." I asked her why, and she said, "People today don't want the recipe unless they can do it in three minutes." I said, "I'm sorry." I do my own cooking when I'm home, and I do it the old-fashioned way. It takes me a little while to cook, but I know what I'm fixing, and it doesn't bother me.

Today, I feel that most everybody can open up a can or open up a box. But when I go home, I cook. And I don't cook like that. It's much, much better if it's homemade.

I love to cook. I love to make bread. If I'm home and I've got somebody coming for dinner, I'm going to have it done. When Jack and Meg White from the White Stripes came down to the house before we started working on my album *Van Lear Rose*, that morning I made four loaves of bread. When Jack left, he said, "That's the best bread I've ever eaten in my life." Sonofagun, if the last time he was out, he didn't say, "Did you bake any bread?"

I want you all to know this cookbook was a total accident. I never set out to write a cookbook, but a year or so ago I started writing down some of my recipes handed down to me from my mommy and from Doo's mom, Angie Lynn. I wanted to give them to my kids and let them pass them down to their kids like my mommy done for me.

I've always included a little story about each recipe or a memory that had to do with a certain dish. I think it is important to pass along memories. My kids thought this was the greatest gift in the world, and so did my manager, Nancy Russell.

She called me up on the phone and asked me if I would be interested in turning these recipes and stories into a cookbook, so that's what we did.

If you want a really good old homemade meal and you want to do it right, if you pay attention to this cookbook, you'll make it. If you don't, then you're liable to do like me. You'll have to try it three or four times, get it thrown out and get run off. The worst happened to me, so I know now.

Of course, I wasn't old enough to know how to cook to begin with. I was just thirteen years old when I got married to Doolittle Lynn. Doo threw out my cooking for at least six months. He run me off and told me I couldn't cook. That taught me a whole bunch. I learned how to cook pretty fast. After six months, he began eating it.

PREFACE

When I got to cooking, Doo loved just about everything that I fixed. I would cook around the stuff that he really liked, like the roast and steak. After we got to making a little money, he had to have meat with every meal. Before that, it was possum or rabbit. Or hamburger. We could get hamburger now and then. But at first we couldn't. It was bad, but we made it.

After we moved to the state of Washington, and I started cooking, Doo would always say, "I'll put my cook up against anybody's!" So he really liked my cooking. He said he taught me everything I know about cooking. Ha! He told me once, "You're one of the best cooks I've ever seen." I thought that was good, coming from him.

I'm not a pretty cook. But my cooking tastes better than it looks. Doolittle would look at it sometimes and go, "Woman, what in the hell have you cooked?" I'd say, "Well, it's a such and such." "Well, it don't look like it to me." But he kind of dived into it when I put it on the table.

I enjoy making things good. If it turns out good, I love it. If it turns out not really good, then I don't like it, you know. I've got to look at the recipe just a little better. I may have to try them three or four times before they turn out, but my daughter Patsy says some of my best creations come from my mistakes.

Usually, I don't go by recipes. I cook like my mommy—a pinch of salt, a pinch of this, and a pinch of that. I taste everything as I go along, to see if I got enough salt in it. Sometimes it works, and sometimes it don't. That's why, before it's ready, I make sure I'm tasting of it.

If I make something and it looks good, it probably doesn't taste good. Doo learned that early on. The night we met, he bought a pie that I had made for a pie social. I had made this chocolate pie, and it looked good to me. But I had made it with salt instead of sugar.

PREFACE

It's important that you pay attention to what your mother's teaching you as you grow up. Mothers have the good recipes, and folks don't make things like they used to, you know.

When I lived in the state of Washington, there was this old lady named Blanche Green. I helped her with the cooking and with cleaning the house for these two bachelors, her nephews. That's how I got my rent paid for. I learned a lot from her. I would say I learned as much from her as I did Mommy. Mommy never had the food to cook like Blanche Green had. Our family had pork, and we had chicken now and then. Outside of that, it was taters and beans, friends. If it wasn't for taters and beans, I wouldn't be sitting here writing to you.

We eat anything and everything we could find in Butcher Holler, Kentucky. Daddy's favorite dish was possum. I would get so mad, because I didn't care for possum that well. I loved rabbit. In fact, I had a rabbit the last night I seen Patsy Cline. Squirrel's one of my favorites, too. When you don't have nothing to eat, things are pretty hard to come by, and possum and rabbit tastes pretty good.

If you want to try possum, I'll teach you how to make it just like Mommy did. Mommy'd always cook that possum until it got tender. There'd be grease an inch thick on it. She'd pour off the water and grease and lay sweet potatoes all around the possum in her baking pan. That was Daddy's favorite food.

I hope all of you enjoy this book. I never had measured anything in my life, so I can't promise it will all turn out. If it don't, blame Nancy, since this was her idea.

I also want to thank William Smithson, Michael McCall, Tim Cobb, and all my kids for helping get everything together for this book.

Love you,
Loretta

★ YOU'RE COOKIN' IT ★ COUNTRY ★

MY FAVORITE RECIPES AND MEMORIES

★ BREAKFAST ★

BUTTERMILK BISCUITS

CAT-HEAD BISCUITS

COUNTRY SAUSAGE GRAVY

OZARK MOUNTAIN BREAKFAST

COUNTRY MORNIN' BREAKFAST CASSEROLE

HASHBROWN CASSEROLE

SAUSAGE PINWHEELS

SCOTCH EGGS

SPANISH OMELET

HOMINY GRITS

SUNRISE BREAKFAST OATMEAL

CORNMEAL MUSH

PIZZA BREAKFAST

CHOCOLATE GRAVY

BUTTERMILK BISCUITS

MAKES 12 SERVINGS

2	CUPS SELF-RISING FLOUR
6	TABLESPOONS SHORTENING
	DASH OF SALT
¾	CUP BUTTERMILK
½	STICK BUTTER

Preheat the oven to 425°. In a large mixing bowl mix the flour, shortening, and salt together. Work in the shortening with a fork until it looks like meal. Add just enough buttermilk to make a nice stiff dough. If it gets too sticky, add just a little more flour, but do not overwork the dough. Touch it as little as possible. Roll out onto a floured board ¼ to ½ inch thick. Cut out biscuits with a floured coffee cup and place on an ungreased baking sheet. Bake until golden brown. Remove from the oven and top each biscuit with a pat of butter.

VARIATION: THESE BISCUITS CAN ALSO BE BAKED IN A CAST-IRON SKILLET IF YOU LIKE 'EM EXTRA CRISPY ON THE SIDES.

DOOLITTLE'S
CAT-HEAD BISCUITS

Doo could cook anything. He was a better cook than I was, I think. He loved to make dressings for chickens and ducks and geese. He loved goose. If I went to town, he'd say, "If you find a nice goose, get it so we can fix it." He loved that, and turkey. He was cooking Chinese stuff for me all the time. He would cook that every night, just about.

Doo would make these great big ol' biscuits. He called them Cat-Head Biscuits. I always made the smaller ones, and he'd say, "Woman, if you're going to stay around here, you're going to have to make Cat-Head Biscuits." The kids loved them. They got to getting up in the morning, saying, "Daddy, you gonna make any Cat-Head Biscuits this morning?"

He didn't roll them out like I roll my biscuits out. I roll mine where they're pretty. He just dipped them out with a spoon, and he said they tasted just the same. He'd drop them in a great big ol' pan that he threw in the oven. There'd be like four or five big spoonfuls that he'd drop for one biscuit. His biscuits would be like two of my biscuits. That's why they're called Cat-Head Biscuits. They're about the size of a cat's head.

CAT-HEAD BISCUITS

MAKES 12 BISCUITS

2	CUPS SELF-RISING FLOUR
1	CUP SHORTENING (CRISCO)
¾	CUP BUTTERMILK

Preheat the oven to 400°. In a large bowl mix the flour and shortening together. With a fork cut the shortening into the flour and add the buttermilk. Stir until the dough leaves the sides of the bowl. Place the dough onto a lightly floured surface. Knead until smooth. Roll out the dough to about ½ inch thick. Cut with a biscuit cutter and arrange on a greased baking sheet. If you don't have a biscuit cutter, you can use the top of a drinking glass. If you're in a hurry and don't care if they look pretty, you can drop them by spoonfuls onto a greased baking sheet to get the authentic Cat-Head Biscuits. Bake for 15 minutes or until nice and brown.

COUNTRY SAUSAGE GRAVY

MAKES 12 SERVINGS

6 to 8	SAUSAGE PATTIES
1	TABLESPOON ALL-PURPOSE FLOUR
1	CUP MILK
	SALT AND PEPPER

In a skillet fry all the sausage patties over medium heat until cooked through. Remove from the skillet and set aside. Stir the flour into the sausage drippings. Slowly add the milk, and salt and pepper to taste. Stir constantly and add more milk if necessary. Crumble the cooked sausage into the gravy mixture. Continue stirring until the gravy is rich and creamy. Serve over toast or biscuits.

OZARK MOUNTAIN BREAKFAST

MAKES 4 SERVINGS

3	TABLESPOONS BUTTER
1	SMALL ONION, CHOPPED
⅓	CUP CHOPPED GREEN PEPPER
1	CUP CHOPPED SMOKED HAM
6	EGGS, SLIGHTLY BEATEN
½	CUP MILK
	TABASCO SAUCE

Melt the butter in a large skillet over medium heat. Sauté the onions, green pepper, and ham in the butter. In a small bowl mix the eggs, milk, and Tabasco to taste. Pour the egg mixture into the skillet. Add the sautéed vegetables and gently scramble for 2 to 3 minutes or until set. Serve with hot biscuits (See buttermilk biscuits recipe on page 3).

Loretta's sons Ernest Ray and Jack.

COUNTRY MORNIN' BREAKFAST CASSEROLE

MAKES 12 SERVINGS

1	POUND PORK SAUSAGE
6	SLICES WHITE BREAD, CUBED
1	CUP SHREDDED CHEDDAR CHEESE
1	CUP SHREDDED SWISS CHEESE
8	LARGE EGGS
2	CUPS HEAVY CREAM
2	CUPS MILK
1	TEASPOON DRIED SAGE
1	TEASPOON SALT
1	TEASPOON PEPPER
1	TEASPOON DRY MUSTARD

In a large skillet over medium heat cook the sausage until done. Drain on paper towels. Crumble the sausage and set aside. Layer the bread, cheddar cheese, Swiss cheese, and sausage in a lightly greased 13 x 9-inch casserole dish to make two layers of each. In a large bowl combine the eggs, cream, milk, sage, salt, pepper, and dry mustard and beat well. Pour the egg mixture evenly over the casserole. Cover and refrigerate overnight. Preheat the oven to 350° and bake for 1 hour or until set. Serve warm.

HASHBROWN CASSEROLE

MAKES 12 SERVINGS

1	(30-OUNCE) BAG FROZEN HASHBROWNS
8	OUNCES SOUR CREAM
1	($10\frac{3}{4}$-OUNCE) CAN CREAM OF CHICKEN SOUP
2	CUPS SHREDDED CHEDDAR CHEESE

Preheat the oven to 350°. In a large bowl mix the hashbrowns, sour cream, chicken soup, and cheese. Place the mixture in a buttered 13 x 9-inch baking dish. Bake for 1 hour.

Loretta in Washington in the 1950s.

LORETTA'S MOMMY

When Mommy cooked, she always baked cornbread or biscuits. Always biscuits in the morning. Mommy had to get up at four o'clock. I would always wake up when she got up. I would lay there in bed, because us kids would go back to sleep. I would know I was going to have to get up and go to school. Mommy would get up and put coffee on for Daddy. Then she would make gravy.

Mommy was a great cook, but she didn't have much to work with. She taught me everything I know. She always taught me about what she was cooking, but it didn't blossom out to fancy dishes. But she knew how to cook them beans and fry them taters and gravy. And eggs, we had eggs. Mommy would always keep a few chickens for eggs. But we didn't have a whole lot.

Mommy worked on an old coal stove, but it was cool. She had a place where she put her flour and meal. She had to have potatoes for fried potatoes . . . and cornbread. She always needed beans. All summer long, she would can. She would put her whole garden up, trying to save for the winter. She'd put potatoes and cabbage heads and stuff into the ground. Then she'd have me cover it with straw. Then I'd put dirt on top of that. It seemed like she would work all summer long, but it would get pretty lean as spring started coming around.

Somehow she always had hog meat to go in the beans. Daddy would kill a hog for Christmas, and he'd salt down the meat. I'd keep running out barefooted while Daddy was scraping the hog. He'd catch me out there and run me back in the house. After Daddy cut the hog meat, Mommy would fry it and make gravy with the scrap. She always kept the hog meat skin, so she could throw that into the beans if she didn't have no pork left. So then biscuits, the gravy, the hog meat, and jam was what you got.

She'd kill a chicken every now and then, and we'd have fried chicken. But that was maybe once a month. Us kids would think we were in heaven when we got a chicken, 'cause we eat beans and taters about every day. It was rough in the hills of Kentucky—it was the good ole days when things were bad.

I remember her trying to help me make biscuits. I made them while she had a baby. Of course, I was thirteen years old. Mommy said for us to leave while the doctor brought the

10

baby, so we went to Grandpa's so the doctor could come and give her that baby. We didn't know anything about it. When I come back, Mommy told me, "Now, Loretta, you're going to have to make the biscuits and fry the hog meat in the morning and make the gravy and everything." Well, I didn't know anything about this, so my first try at it, I went and had to pour out the gravy. I didn't want Daddy to see me, so I tried it again. This was a mess. I took the flour and stuff into the bed, and Mommy showed me what to do. And the biscuits wasn't that bad, but they wasn't that good either. It was one of them times. But when

Mommy got up out of the bed where she could teach me how to do that, that was the first thing she done, is to teach me how to make gravy and biscuits and stuff like that.

Mommy was always dancin' and singin' and carrying on when I was home. She loved Roy Acuff, and she loved Ernest Tubb. But Mommy knew songs that they had made up in the hills of Kentucky, and these are the songs that she taught me. Like, if a girl got pregnant, well, there was a song wrote about it. If the girl was going with somebody, you might as well hang it up if

Loretta's mom, Clara Webb, at age 33.

11

something happened to her. That's who they would get. There wasn't no court. If something happened to the daughter, the father would go after them. There wasn't no playing around up there.

But Mommy danced and sang all the time. You know, the only thing I didn't like about the movie *Coal Miner's Daughter* was how drab they dressed the lady who played Mommy. Mommy dressed in colors. She loved colors. She would dye them feed sacks. We wore the dadgummest colors you ever seen in your life. She was real colorful.

I made sure that they pretty well stuck by how they were making the movie, but I didn't know they were going to dress her so drab. Mommy, she said, "Now, that's just fine, Loretty." But I felt really bad, because I should've been watching a little bit better.

She was a great mommy. We lost her from smoking cigarettes. She got cancer of the lungs. But, my goodness, she was a good person. I think we had the best mommy in the world.

SAUSAGE PINWHEELS

MAKES 8 (2-SLICE) SERVINGS

1	POUND SAUSAGE
8	OUNCES CREAM CHEESE
2	(8-COUNT) CANS CRESCENT ROLLS

In a skillet fry the sausage over medium heat until done. Chop finely. In a large bowl combine the cream cheese and sausage. Unroll the dough and press the perforations together to form a rectangle. Spread the sausage mixture over the dough. Roll up tightly and wrap the mixture in plastic wrap. Chill for 1 hour. Preheat the oven to 350°. Remove the plastic wrap and slice the roll-up into 1-inch slices. Arrange the slices on a baking sheet and bake for 10 to 12 minutes.

SCOTCH EGGS

MAKES 6 SERVINGS

1	POUND BULK PORK SAUSAGE
6	HARD-BOILED EGGS, PEELED
2	EGGS, BEATEN
1	CUP ITALIAN SEASONED BREADCRUMBS
	VEGETABLE OIL FOR FRYING

Fill a deep fryer half full with vegetable oil. Heat to 375°. Divide the sausage into six equal portions. Press each into a thin patty and form around a hard-boiled egg, sealing completely. Dip each sausage-enclosed egg in the beaten eggs and roll in the breadcrumbs. Fry in the hot oil for 7 to 9 minutes or until the sausage is done. Drain well on paper towels. Let cool to room temperature. Cut the eggs in half and serve.

SPANISH OMELET

MAKES 4 SERVINGS

3	EGGS
2	TABLESPOONS MILK
$\frac{1}{4}$	TEASPOON ONION POWDER
$\frac{1}{8}$	TEASPOON SALT
$\frac{1}{2}$	CUP SLICED FRESH MUSHROOMS
2	TABLESPOONS CHOPPED GREEN BELL PEPPER
8	($\frac{1}{2}$-INCH-THICK) TOMATO SLICES
4	ENGLISH MUFFINS, SPLIT AND TOASTED
$\frac{1}{4}$	CUP SHREDDED CHEDDAR CHEESE
$\frac{1}{8}$	TEASPOON BLACK PEPPER

In a bowl combine the eggs, milk, onion powder, and salt. Whisk until blended. Coat a medium skillet with cooking spray and heat over medium-high heat until hot. Add the mushrooms and green pepper and sauté until tender. Reduce the heat. Add the egg mixture and cook until the mixture is set but still moist, stirring occasionally. Place a tomato slice on each English muffin half. Top each with 2 tablespoons of the egg mixture and $\frac{1}{2}$ tablespoon of the cheese. Sprinkle with the pepper. Place the muffins on a baking sheet and broil six inches from the heat for 1 minute or until the cheese melts.

HOMINY GRITS

MAKES 8 SERVINGS

4	CUPS WATER
1	CUP HOMINY GRITS
1	POUND SHARP CHEDDAR CHEESE, GRATED
3	EGGS, BEATEN
2	TEASPOONS SALT
1	TABLESPOON TABASCO
1	TEASPOON PAPRIKA
1½	STICKS BUTTER

Preheat the oven to 250°. Bring the water to a boil in a saucepan. Add the grits and cook until thick, stirring occasionally. In a large bowl combine the cheese, eggs, salt, Tabasco, paprika, and butter. Stir the cheese mixture into the grits. Pour into an 11 x 8-inch baking pan and bake for 1 hour. Cut into squares and serve.

SUNRISE BREAKFAST OATMEAL

MAKES 6 SERVINGS

$2\frac{1}{4}$	CUPS QUICK-COOKING OATS
$\frac{3}{4}$	CUP FIRMLY PACKED BROWN SUGAR
$\frac{3}{4}$	CUP RAISINS
1	TEASPOON GROUND CINNAMON
$\frac{1}{2}$	TEASPOON SALT
$3\frac{1}{3}$	CUPS MILK
4	EGG WHITES, LIGHTLY BEATEN
1	TABLESPOON VEGETABLE OIL
1	TEASPOON VANILLA EXTRACT

Preheat the oven to 350°. Coat an 8-inch square glass baking dish with cooking spray. In a large bowl combine the oats, brown sugar, raisins, cinnamon, and salt and mix well. In a medium bowl, combine the milk, egg whites, oil, and vanilla and mix well. Add the milk mixture to the dry ingredients and mix. Pour into the baking dish and bake for 55 to 60 minutes or until the center is set and firm to the touch. Cool slightly. Serve with fruit. Leftovers can be refrigerated in a tightly covered container.

JOHNNY AND JUNE CARTER CASH

When I first come to Nashville, the Carter family tried to get me to join them because I looked so much like Anita and June Carter. Mother Maybelle Carter said, "Well, you look enough like my girls to pass in the Carter family." I said, "No, I want to make it on my own, you know. I want to do it by myself." Of course, June never did let me forget that. But Johnny Cash always thought me and June looked a lot alike. Then some people would say, "No, it's you and Anita." I said, "Forget it; I look like the Carter family. Don't worry about which one." It was a good decision, though, or I'd never have made it by myself.

Any time we got together, June and I would act the fool. Johnny would tell us, "Settle it down, girls," but we had a good time. We never had a long time together unless we were on the road. If we were on the road, we'd spend some time at a restaurant or something like that.

When we had a long time off, I'd go to Hawaii or the Bahamas, and they'd go to Jamaica. I said, "Could we do something, maybe get in one big house? One of us live upstairs and the other one down, and us get together on vacation?" You know, we were talking about that before John got sick.

John and June, they were really close, and they were pretty close to God. That's one thing that I thank God about. They give me a pin that came from the Holy Land to go on the Coal Miner's Daughter dress. It's whitish, all marble-looking, and it has the disciples on top. The rest of it is sprayed with platinum gold. I tried to get somebody to tell me how much it was worth. Because of the condition it was in and where it comes from and because it was made with such great pains, they said they couldn't even figure out how much it was worth. I never could get it appraised.

The last time I really seen them, I was in the hospital. They come and they prayed with me. Every time I would hit the hospital for exhaustion or whatever, John and June were the first ones there. After they got religion—this was really a big thing to them—they'd come in and pray. I'm glad I do have memories like that.

I talked to June a few days before she passed away. She was just leaving her house, so the phone rang about five times. I thought, "Well, she's not at home." I had called her just as she started to close the door, going back to the hospital. I said, "I didn't know if you was home. You didn't answer the phone right away." She said, "I had to run back in because I'm going to see Johnny." I said, "Well, I'm glad I caught you. I was calling to tell you to go out and tell Johnny how much I love him because I haven't gotten to come up and see him. I've been on the road." And I said, "I want you to know that I love you."

She said, "Oh, Lord, I'll do this as soon as I get there. It'll just tickle John to death." Bless her little heart. I didn't know she was going to have anything done.

I was shocked; I'll tell you that. Talking to her an' her not telling me anything was the matter with her. I don't think she wanted to tell me. She didn't want me to know. It tore me all to pieces, because we were so close. It just tore me all to pieces.

CORNMEAL MUSH

MAKES 4 SERVINGS

1	CUP GROUND CORNMEAL
1	CUP COLD WATER
1	TEASPOON SALT

Heat the cornmeal, water, and salt in a double boiler over 4 cups of boiling water. Cook over high heat for 2 to 3 minutes, stirring once. Reduce the heat slightly. Cover and let the mixture steam over boiling water for 15 to 25 minutes longer, stirring frequently. Serve with butter, honey, or raw sugar.

Loretta as a teenager in Kentucky in the 1940s.

PIZZA BREAKFAST

MAKES 8 SERVINGS

1	POUND BULK PORK SAUSAGE
1	(8-OUNCE) PACKAGE CRESCENT DINNER ROLLS
1	CUP SHREDDED SHARP CHEDDAR CHEESE
6	EGGS, BEATEN
$\frac{1}{2}$	CUP MILK
$\frac{3}{4}$	TEASPOON DRIED OREGANO
$\frac{1}{8}$	TEASPOON PEPPER

Preheat the oven to 375°. Brown the sausage in a skillet over medium heat, stirring until crumbly, and then drain. Separate the rolls into triangles. Arrange on a greased 12-inch pizza pan with the points toward the center. Press to seal. Bake for 5 minutes on the lower oven rack. Remove from the oven and reduce the temperature to 350°. Spread the sausage over the crust. In a medium bowl mix the cheese, eggs, milk, oregano, and pepper together. Pour over the sausage. Bake for 30 to 40 minutes.

CHOCOLATE GRAVY

MAKES 6 SERVINGS

1	CUP SUGAR
4	TABLESPOONS ALL-PURPOSE FLOUR
	PINCH OF SALT
2	TABLESPOONS COCOA
3	CUPS WHOLE MILK OR HALF-AND-HALF
½	STICK BUTTER
1	TEASPOON VANILLA EXTRACT

In a saucepan combine the sugar, flour, salt, and cocoa and cook over medium heat. Gradually add the milk. Cook until thick and creamy, stirring frequently. Remove from the heat and stir in the butter and vanilla. Serve over biscuits.

★ SNACKS ★

BEEF PARTY SNACKS

CRAB DIP

BLT DIP

WHITE BEAN DIP

FRIED PICKLES

PIMIENTO CHEESE

CHEESE STRAWS

TASTE OF THE ORIENT PARTY MIX

HAM ROLLS

PIGS IN A BLANKET

SWEET & SMOKEY SAUSAGES

SAUSAGE BALLS

OLD TIMEY POPCORN BALLS

FRIED BOLOGNA SANDWICHES

DEVILED HAM & TUNA SANDWICHES

BEEF PARTY SNACKS

MAKES 24 SNACKS

1	POUND GROUND BEEF
1	POUND SAUSAGE
2	TEASPOONS DRIED OREGANO
1	POUND VELVEETA CHEESE, SHREDDED
1	LOAF PARTY RYE BREAD

Preheat the oven to 350°. In a skillet over medium heat brown the ground beef and sausage together. Drain well and stir in the oregano and cheese. Place the bread slices on a baking sheet and spoon some mixture onto each slice. Bake until warmed through, about 10 minutes.

CRAB DIP

MAKES 12 SERVINGS

8	OUNCES CREAM CHEESE, SOFTENED
8	OUNCES MAYONNAISE
	SALT AND PEPPER
1	POUND LUMP CRABMEAT
1	(8-OUNCE) JAR COCKTAIL SAUCE

In a large bowl combine the cream cheese and mayonnaise. Add the salt and pepper to taste. Gently mix in the crabmeat, taking care not to break it up too much. Line a bowl with plastic wrap. Spoon the dip into the bowl and chill until the dip becomes firm, about 45 minutes. Invert the dip onto a serving plate and remove the plastic wrap. Pour the cocktail sauce evenly over the dip. Serve with crackers.

BLT DIP

MAKES 12 SERVINGS

1	POUND BACON
8	OUNCES SOUR CREAM
8	OUNCES MAYONNAISE
	SALT AND PEPPER
1	HEAD LETTUCE
$\frac{1}{2}$	CUP CHOPPED TOMATOES

In a skillet over medium-high heat fry the bacon until crisp. Crumble the bacon and set aside. In a medium bowl combine the sour cream and mayonnaise. Stir in the bacon and salt and pepper to taste. Line a serving bowl with lettuce leaves. Spoon the dip into the lettuce-lined bowl and top with the chopped tomatoes. Chill in refrigerator for about 1 hour. Serve with crackers.

WHITE BEAN DIP

MAKES 8 SERVINGS

2	CUPS COOKED WHITE BEANS
1	GARLIC CLOVE
2	TABLESPOONS CHOPPED ROSEMARY
1	TABLESPOON TAHINI
2	TABLESPOONS RED PEPPER FLAKES
	DASH OF SALT
½ to ¾	CUP OLIVE OIL

Combine the beans, garlic, rosemary, tahini, red pepper flakes, and salt in the work bowl of a food processor. Gradually add the olive oil while pulsing until it is well blended and smooth. Serve with pita toast points.

DOO'S DAD CLEANS HOUSE

Pop—that's what we called Doo's dad, Red—came up to stay with us once while we were living in the state of Washington. Pop and I would spend all day playing pinochle. I'd put something on for supper, and when it was almost time for Doo to come home, that's when the dishes would get washed and all the housework would get done. Pop would start cleaning the house, and I'd start washing the dishes. Pop would do the sweeping, but what I didn't know was that he was raising up a corner of the linoleum and sweeping everything under it.

One day, Doo came in and he seen a hump in the floor. He raised the linoleum up and there was this great big pile of dirt. He thought it was me. He thought I was doing that, so he jumped all over me.

"You leave her alone," Pop told Doo. "I put that dirt under there."

"Why did you put it under there?" Doo asked him.

"It's cold," Pop said. "I didn't want to go outside and get the dustpan."

FRIED PICKLES

MAKES 6 SERVINGS

	VEGETABLE OIL FOR FRYING
1	CUP ALL-PURPOSE FLOUR
1	CUP CORNMEAL
1	(16-OUNCE) JAR DILL PICKLE CHIPS, DRAINED

Pour enough oil into a skillet to measure 2 to 3 inches deep. Heat the oil to 350°. In a bowl combine the flour and cornmeal. Dredge the pickles in the flour mixture. Fry the pickles in the hot oil until golden brown. Remove from the oil and drain on paper towels.

Loretta and Doo at Hurricane Mills in the late 1980s.

PIMIENTO CHEESE

MAKES 8 SERVINGS

1	POUND AMERICAN CHEESE, SHREDDED
8	OUNCES MAYONNAISE
1	SMALL ONION, FINELY CHOPPED
	SALT AND PEPPER
1	(2-OUNCE) JAR PIMIENTOS

In a large bowl combine the cheese, mayonnaise, and onion. Add salt and pepper to taste. Gently fold in the pimientos. Serve with crackers or make sandwiches.

CHEESE STRAWS

MAKES 4 DOZEN

2	CUPS SHARP CHEDDAR CHEESE, GRATED
2	CUPS ALL-PURPOSE FLOUR
1	CUP MELTED BUTTER
4	EGGS, BEATEN

Preheat the oven to 375°. In a bowl mix the cheese, flour, and butter. Stir thoroughly. Combine the eggs with the cheese mixture. With a rolling pin, roll the mixture to about a ½-inch thickness. Cut into ½ x 3-inch strips. Spray a baking sheet with cooking spray. Place the strips on the sheet. Bake for 10 minutes or until brown. Cool before serving. Store in an airtight container.

TASTE OF THE ORIENT PARTY MIX

MAKES 10 SERVINGS

1	CUP UNSALTED ROASTED PEANUTS
2	CUPS CHOW MEIN NOODLES
$1\frac{1}{4}$	CUPS SQUARE RICE CEREAL
$2\frac{1}{2}$	TABLESPOONS MELTED BUTTER
1	TABLESPOON SOY SAUCE
$\frac{1}{4}$	TEASPOON CELERY SALT
$\frac{1}{4}$	TEASPOON GARLIC POWDER

Preheat the oven to 250°. In a large bowl combine the peanuts, noodles, and cereal. In a small bowl combine the butter, soy sauce, celery salt, and garlic powder. Mix well. Pour the butter mixture over the noodle mixture, tossing to coat evenly. Spread on ungreased baking sheets and bake for 30 minutes. Let cool for 30 minutes. Store in airtight containers.

HAM ROLLS

MAKES 12 SERVINGS

8	OUNCES CREAM CHEESE, SOFTENED
1	(16-OUNCE) PACKAGE SLICED BAKED HAM

Spread the cream cheese over the ham slices. Roll up tightly and refrigerate for 1 hour. Slice the ham rolls into bite-size pieces and serve.

*Jack, Ernest Ray, and Loretta
in Washington in the early 1960s.*

PIGS IN A BLANKET

MAKES 12 SERVINGS

1 (8-COUNT) CAN REFRIGERATED CRESCENT ROLLS
1 (12-OUNCE) PACKAGE "LITTLE SMOKIES" SAUSAGES

Preheat the oven to 350°. Unroll the dough and cut into small triangles. Wrap each sausage with a dough triangle and arrange on a baking sheet. Bake for 10 minutes. Serve with spicy mustard.

SWEET & SMOKEY SAUSAGES

MAKES 12 SERVINGS

2	(12-OUNCE) PACKAGES "LITTLE SMOKIES" SAUSAGES
1	(12-OUNCE) JAR GRAPE JELLY
1	(18-OUNCE) BOTTLE BARBECUE SAUCE

In a slow cooker combine the sausages, jelly, and barbecue sauce. Cook on high for about 1 hour or on low for about 2 hours. Serve hot.

SAUSAGE BALLS

MAKES 12 SERVINGS

1	POUND RAW PORK SAUSAGE
2	CUPS SHREDDED CHEDDAR CHEESE
2	CUPS BAKING MIX (BISQUICK)

Preheat the oven to 350°. In a large bowl mix the sausage, cheese, and baking mix. Shape the mixture into 2-inch balls and arrange on a baking sheet. Bake for 12 to 15 minutes. Serve hot.

OLD TIMEY POPCORN BALLS

MAKES 12 SERVINGS

This is a fun and easy recipe to include the whole family in the making.

12	CUPS COOKED POPCORN (ABOUT 6 TABLESPOONS KERNELS)
$\frac{1}{2}$	TEASPOON SALT
2	TABLESPOONS BUTTER
1	CUP MOLASSES
$\frac{1}{2}$	CUP SUGAR

Combine the popcorn and salt in a large bowl. Melt the butter in a small pan over medium heat. Add the molasses and sugar. Cook, stirring frequently, until the mixture becomes brittle when dropped into water. While the mixture is still hot, pour over the popcorn and mix together. Shape into balls.

NOTE: RUB BUTTER ON YOUR HANDS TO PREVENT THE POPCORN FROM STICKING TO THEM.

PICKING BERRIES

We knew where all the blackberries were in Butcher Holler. There was a big patch of them just up the hill from our house. From year to year, we'd go pick. Mommy would tell us, "Now, tie your pants legs. Put elastic around them so the chiggers won't get you." Man, I'd be eat up with them chiggers, no matter what I would do.

My first cousin Marie Castle always went blackberry picking with us. One day, we'd been out for a while, and I got tired. I said, "Let's just lay down for a few minutes before we pick up our buckets and go home." She said okay, so I laid down. I wasn't paying any attention to what I was doing. I laid my head down and said, "Marie, this is the softest pillow I have ever slept on." She said, "Loretta, your head is full of cow manure." I had laid down in this fresh pile of cow manure! I could not believe it.

Mommy wouldn't let me come in the house. She brought a big tub of water out for me to wash my hair. It was good that it was a warm day. She made me stay out until I got clean. That was one memorable time that I'd just as soon forgot. But you can't forget that.

Daddy's favorite berries was blueberries. We had a patch of huckleberries on top of the hill. Huckleberries look like blueberries, only they're bigger. So I was going to be good to Daddy one day. Me and Marie went out picking berries again. We went up the hill, and I got a bucket almost full. We started home, and we started down the hill. As I started to step down, there was a big copperhead coiled up and ready to strike me. I went up over the top of that copperhead, and I spilled every berry I had. But I didn't get bit.

I went home crying. I said, "Daddy, I had a whole bucket of berries for you." "Yeah, yeah," he said. Daddy didn't believe me. But that bucket was full of huckleberries.

Another time, I had took a whole pail of wild raspberries I had picked to the back of my bus. I woke up in the middle of the night and ate that whole pail of raspberries. I didn't pay any attention to my face, I just kept eating with my eyes closed, and then I went back to sleep. When I woke up that morning, them raspberry stains was all over everything— my hands, my face. I thought it was blood. I hollered for the bus driver. I said, "I'm bleeding to death, and I don't know where the blood's coming from!" So he stopped the bus and came back. He started looking around, and he saw the pail where the raspberries had been, and he said, "Damn, Loretta! You've eat the raspberries, and they're all over the place!" I felt pretty foolish, but it was better than bleeding to death.

FRIED BOLOGNA SANDWICHES

MAKES 1 SERVING

I know some of you are sayin' "What the heck is a fried bologna sandwich."
Just try it. Believe me, you're gonna love it.

1	SLICE BOLOGNA
2	SLICES BREAD
	TRIMMINGS OF YOUR CHOICE

In a skillet fry the bologna over medium heat until brown on each side. Dress the slices of bread with all the trimmings. Add the fried bologna, and you have a fried bologna sandwich.

NOTE: WHEN FRYING THE BOLOGNA MAKE A FEW CUTS IN IT SO IT WILL VENT AND LIE FLAT.

DEVILED HAM & TUNA SANDWICHES

MAKES 8 SERVINGS

1	(6½-OUNCE) CAN TUNA, DRAINED AND FLAKED
1	(4½-OUNCE) CAN DEVILED HAM
3	HARD-BOILED EGGS, CHOPPED
¼	CUP FINELY CHOPPED CELERY
2	TABLESPOONS CHOPPED DILL PICKLE
½	TEASPOON GRATED ONION
⅓	CUP MIRACLE WHIP OR MAYONNAISE
16	SLICES WHITE BREAD
	SOFTENED BUTTER
8	LETTUCE LEAVES

In a bowl combine the tuna, deviled ham, eggs, celery, pickle, and onion. Stir in the Miracle Whip and chill in the refrigerator until ready to serve. When ready to serve, spread 8 slices of the bread with butter. Spread the tuna mixture over the butter. Place a lettuce leaf and the remaining bread slices on top. Cut in half or serve whole.

DOO'S FAMILY

My daddy and Doo's mother were distant cousins, but Doo's family had been living in the state of Washington before they moved to Kentucky, just two hollers over from us. Hollers were like streets nowadays only hollers are muddier. Red and Angie, Doo's parents, had ten kids. Doo was the oldest, and he had joined the army. But the rest of the kids went to our school.

We heard this new family was coming to go to school at our little one-room schoolhouse. All the kids was excited. There were only twenty-eight or twenty-nine kids in the whole school, you know, so it was really something to get somebody that you didn't know. And the Lynns had ten kids.

Doo's mom was a great cook. Angie had worked as a cook for one of the hotels in Washington state. It didn't matter whether she had ten dollars to cook with that day, or a hundred dollars, she always made a great meal. She made angel food cakes for people in the hollers that was getting married, and sometimes she'd cook food for the miners.

Red always grew a big garden, and Angie always put up a lot of good food. Angie would can everything, not only vegetables but meats, too, like pork and beef. They always had a little cellar out there near their house. Every time somebody would come over to Angie's house—some of the ten kids, or if the grandkids would come over—she'd start complaining, "Oh, I didn't know all of y'all were coming; I don't have enough food." She'd go on and on while she was scooting around the kitchen. The whole time people were sitting there eating, she'd be talking about how there wasn't enough and how she wished it would be better. Meanwhile, she'd put a meal on the table that was fit for a king.

SOUPS, ★ SALADS & ★ RELISHES

HARVEST SOUP

COUNTRY CABBAGE SOUP

CABBAGE SOUP

VAN LEAR VEGETABLE SOUP

PORK & HOMINY SOUP

SOUTHERN STYLE CHILI

CORN CHOWDER

TRADITIONAL TOSSED SALAD

LORETTA'S WILTED LETTUCE

GREEK SALAD

CHICKEN SALAD

CUCUMBER SALAD

PASTA SALAD

POTATO SALAD

RED BEAN SALAD

CARROT & RAISIN SALAD

MUSTARD PICKLES

BEET RELISH

CUCUMBER RELISH

HARVEST SOUP

MAKES 4 SERVINGS

1	POUND GROUND BEEF, COOKED
½	ONION, CHOPPED
4	CUPS WATER
2	POTATOES, CHOPPED
2	CARROTS, CHOPPED
2	TEASPOONS SALT
2	BAY LEAVES
½	TEASPOON BASIL
1	(28-OUNCE) CAN OF TOMATOES, CHOPPED

In a skillet brown the ground beef over medium-high heat just until brown. Drain and place in medium saucepan over medium-high heat. Add the onion and cook for 5 minutes or until tender. Add the water, potatoes, carrots, salt, bay leaves, and basil and bring to a boil. Reduce the heat to medium-low and simmer, covered, for 20 minutes. Stir in the tomatoes and simmer for 5 minutes longer or until heated through.

COUNTRY CABBAGE SOUP

MAKES 6 SERVINGS

1	LARGE CABBAGE, CHOPPED
2	ONIONS, CHOPPED
2	GREEN BELL PEPPERS
2	CELERY STALKS, CHOPPED
3	($14\frac{1}{2}$-OUNCE) CANS TOMATOES, STEWED
1	ENVELOPE ONION SOUP MIX

Put the cabbage, onions, peppers, celery, tomatoes, and soup mix in a large pot. Cook on medium heat for 20 minutes or until the vegetables are tender.

FOOD LINES

I had to stand in the government food lines the first couple years Doo and I lived in Washington state. That was something Mommy had done, too, back in Kentucky. A little later, I got a job cooking and cleaning and taking care of the house for a couple of brothers, and I was pretty well taken care of after that.

I'd take anything I could get from those food lines. I would flirt with the guys. I'd get up on a bank where they could see me, and I'd start hollering—"Throw me a cabbage head! Throw me this! Throw me that!" When you've got four kids, you're going to holler, ain't ya?

It was either that, or we go hungry. If you're married to someone that drinks, you're not going to end up with much at the table unless you work it.

CABBAGE SOUP

MAKES 6 SERVINGS

1	SLICE BACON, CHOPPED
2	MEDIUM GARLIC CLOVES, CRUSHED
1	LARGE ONION, CHOPPED
1	LARGE NEW POTATO, PEELED AND CUBED
$\frac{1}{2}$	TEASPOON DRIED DILL WEED
4	CUPS SHREDDED CABBAGE
2	(14-OUNCE) CANS BEEF BROTH
1	(28-OUNCE) CAN CRUSHED TOMATOES, NOT DRAINED
$1\frac{1}{2}$	CUPS WATER
$\frac{1}{8}$	TEASPOON BLACK PEPPER

In a skillet fry the bacon over medium-high-heat for 4 minutes or until crisp, stirring constantly. Remove the bacon and set aside. Add the garlic, onion, potato, and dill weed to the drippings. Cover and cook for about 5 minutes, stirring occasionally. Stir in the cabbage and cook 5 minutes longer. Add the broth, tomatoes, water, and pepper. Cook until the vegetables are tender-crisp. Ladle the soup into individual bowls and top with the bacon pieces.

VAN LEAR VEGETABLE SOUP

MAKES 6 SERVINGS

1	POUND GROUND BEEF, COOKED
3	CELERY STALKS, CHOPPED
3	CARROTS, CHOPPED
3	POTATOES, DICED
1	ONION, CHOPPED
1	(14½-OUNCE) CAN STEWED TOMATOES
1	(10-OUNCE) CAN TOMATO SAUCE
2	CUPS WATER
1	BEEF BOUILLON CUBE
1	TABLESPOON WORCESTERSHIRE SAUCE
	SALT AND PEPPER

Brown the ground beef in a skillet over medium-high heat. Drain the beef and place in a large saucepan over medium heat. Add the celery, carrots, potatoes, onion, tomatoes, tomato sauce, water, bouillon cube, Worcestershire sauce, and salt and pepper to taste. Cook for 20 minutes or until the vegetables are tender.

PORK & HOMINY SOUP

MAKES 10 TO 12 SERVINGS

2	POUNDS PORK RIBS
1	LARGE ONION, QUARTERED
1	GARLIC CLOVE, PEELED
1	($10\frac{3}{4}$-OUNCE) CAN CHICKEN BROTH
5	CUPS COLD WATER
$\frac{1}{2}$	TEASPOON SALT
$\frac{1}{4}$	TEASPOON PEPPER
2	(16-OUNCE) CANS WHITE HOMINY, RINSED AND DRAINED
	CHILI POWDER
1	CUP SHREDDED LETTUCE
$\frac{1}{2}$	CUP CHOPPED GREEN ONIONS
6	RADISHES, SLICED

In a 5-quart Dutch oven, combine the pork ribs, onion, garlic, chicken broth, water, salt, and pepper over high heat. Bring to a boil. Reduce the heat and simmer, covered, for 1 hour. Add the hominy to the pork mixture and cook for 1 hour longer. Remove the pork ribs from the broth and cool. Shred the meat from the bones and discard the bones. Skim the fat from the broth. Before serving, add chili powder to taste. Cover and simmer for 10 minutes longer. Ladle the soup into bowls and garnish with shredded lettuce, green onions, and radishes.

DINAH SHORE AND THE POTATO SOUP

Every time I went on Dinah Shore's show, we'd feed the whole bunch in the studio. One time, we decided we were going to fix our favorite recipes for everybody in the audience and see which one they liked better. She told me she was going to make potato soup. Everybody loves my chicken and dumplins, so that's what I wanted to make. We started arguing in front of this whole audience about who was going to have the best dish. She told everybody in there: "They won't be worth a thing. I'm from Tennessee, and I know what chicken and dumplins taste like." I said okay.

So we had the studio full of people, and here she was making potato soup. But somebody had turned the dadgum stove on, and she didn't know it was hot. This little cooker was sitting there, and when she poured the potato soup into that thing to get it all hot, it shot clear up to the ceiling. Potato soup went everywhere. It tore her up, because everyone was watching. I felt so sorry for her, but it was the funniest durn thing.

Anyway, I won. Of course, she absolutely hit the roof with her potato soup, so how could it get any better? They wouldn't let me do nothing but chicken and dumplins from that day on.

SOUTHERN STYLE CHILI

MAKES 10 TO 12 SERVINGS

2	TEASPOONS OLIVE OIL
1	MEDIUM ONION, CHOPPED
$1\frac{1}{2}$	POUNDS GROUND BEEF
1	(12-OUNCE) CAN DICED TOMATOES
1	CUP WATER
1	(12-OUNCE) CAN PINTO BEANS
1	(12-OUNCE) CAN KIDNEY BEANS
2	TEASPOONS CHILI POWDER
1	TEASPOON GARLIC POWDER
1	TEASPOON SALT

In a skillet heat the olive oil over medium-high heat and sauté the onion. Add the ground beef and brown. In a large saucepan warm the tomatoes and ½ cup of the water over medium heat for five minutes. Stir occasionally. Add the hamburger mixture to the tomato mixture. Stir in the pinto beans, kidney beans, chili powder, garlic powder, and salt. Simmer on low heat for two hours. Add the remaining water as needed for desired consistency.

THE CHILI CATASTROPHE

One day, when we were living in Washington state and my little sister Peggy Sue had come up to visit, we took a notion that we would make some chili. I'd never made chili before, but everything I did was from scratch. I wouldn't buy canned stuff from the store.

I had got a new pressure cooker that week, so I put the chili in this big pressure cooker. I was going to be really smart and have it all ready when Doo came in for dinner. Of course, I had four kids at the time, so it took quite a bit of chili.

Well, when I got this pressure cooker, I didn't know that you had to let the steam out of it. I didn't read too good at that time. While the chili was cooking, my sister Peggy and I took my guitar, and we sat at the table singing. Peggy Sue was always interested in music, too—later, she wrote "Don't Come Home A-Drinkin' (With Lovin' on Your Mind)" with me. All of a sudden, we heard this racket going on, and that pressure cooker was shaking to beat the band.

When we took the pressure cooker off the stove and took the lid off, the whole dadgum thing hit the top of the ceiling. We had chili all over the kitchen. We even had chili in other rooms of the house.

We never did get rid of all that chili. I don't know who's living in that house now, but I bet there's chili in there still.

CORN CHOWDER

MAKES 10 SERVINGS

2	POUNDS WHITE POTATOES, DICED
1	BAY LEAF
4	CUPS WATER
3	TABLESPOONS BUTTER
3	MEDIUM ONIONS, CHOPPED
4	CELERY RIBS, CHOPPED
1	MEDIUM GREEN BELL PEPPER, CHOPPED
2	TEASPOONS CUMIN SEEDS
2	TABLESPOONS ALL-PURPOSE FLOUR
$\frac{1}{2}$	TEASPOON SAGE
$\frac{1}{2}$	TEASPOON PEPPER
2	CUPS MILK
$1\frac{2}{3}$	CUPS WHOLE KERNEL CORN

In a large saucepan over high heat combine the potatoes, bay leaf, and water. Bring to a boil. Reduce the heat to medium and cook for 10 minutes. Drain, reserving the liquid. Discard the bay leaf. In a soup pot, melt the butter over medium-high heat. Add the onions, celery, green pepper, and cumin seeds. Cook until the onions are tender, stirring constantly. Stir in the flour, sage, and pepper. Stir in enough of the reserved liquid to make a smooth paste. Stir in the remaining liquid and the potatoes. Cook until heated through. Stir in the milk and corn and heat thoroughly.

TRADITIONAL TOSSED SALAD

MAKES 8 SERVINGS

*If you don't like one of the ingredients, you can leave it out or set it aside
in a separate dish, and each person can add the toppings she likes.*

½	POUND BACON
1	HEAD OF LETTUCE, CHOPPED
1	BUNCH OF ROMAINE LETTUCE, CHOPPED
1	CUP GRATED CHEDDAR CHEESE
1	CUP GRATED CARROTS
1	LARGE TOMATO, CHOPPED
1	CUCUMBER, SLICED
½	RED ONION, CHOPPED
10	SMALL RADISHES, SLICED

In a skillet over medium-high heat fry the bacon until crisp. Crumble the bacon and set aside. In a large bowl toss the lettuces, cheese, carrots, tomato, cucumber, onion, and radishes together. Top with salad dressing of your choice and sprinkle the bacon bits on top.

WILD PLANTS

The snow wouldn't hardly be off the ground in Butcher Holler, and you'd see Mommy out with a bucket and a knife picking wild greens. I started going with her. Mommy would pick plantain, watercress, and speckled dock. Speckled dock is green, but it's got little red specks on it. Then there's sour dock. Mommy picked poke sallet, too. Mommy always put one big stalk of poke sallet in the new greens that she was cooking. She would make us poke stalks and fry them like fish, too. They were real good.

So I know everything you can pick that won't kill you. It's been a good dadgum thing, too. After I left home, I found myself hungry a lot of times. When me and my kids got hungry, I knew how Mommy must've felt at times. You don't know unless you put yourself in that place.

LORETTA'S WILTED LETTUCE

MAKES 6 SERVINGS

2	HEADS FRESH LEAF LETTUCE, TORN IN PIECES
2	TABLESPOONS SLICED GREEN ONIONS
2	TABLESPOONS SLICED RADISHES
5	SLICES BACON
$\frac{1}{4}$	TEASPOON SALT
$\frac{1}{4}$	TEASPOON PEPPER
$\frac{1}{4}$	CUP VINEGAR
$1\frac{1}{2}$	TEASPOONS SUGAR
$\frac{1}{8}$	TEASPOON GARLIC SALT (OPTIONAL)

Combine the lettuce, green onions, and radishes in a salad bowl. In a skillet over medium-high heat fry the bacon until crisp. Set aside on paper towels to drain. Add the salt, pepper, vinegar, sugar, and garlic salt to the bacon drippings. Bring to a boil, stirring constantly. Immediately pour the mixture over the salad. Crumble the bacon over the salad and toss well.

GREEK SALAD

MAKES 6 SERVINGS

1	GARLIC CLOVE, CUT IN HALF
2	MEDIUM TOMATOES, CUT IN WEDGES
1	MEDIUM CUCUMBER, PEELED AND SLICED
1	GREEN PEPPER, SLICED
2	GREEN ONIONS, CHOPPED
2	CUPS CRUMBLED FETA CHEESE
12	GREEK OR BLACK OLIVES
6	CUPS TORN ROMAINE LETTUCE

Rub a salad bowl or platter with the garlic. Arrange the tomatoes, cucumber, green pepper, onions, cheese, and olives on a bed of lettuce or toss the ingredients together with lettuce. Add dressing to taste.

VARIATION: ADD 1 OUNCE FLAT ANCHOVY FILLETS TO YOUR SALAD INGREDIENTS.

CHICKEN SALAD

MAKES 8 SERVINGS

2	POUNDS COOKED CHICKEN
$\frac{1}{2}$	CUP MAYONNAISE
$\frac{1}{2}$	CUP MUSTARD
$\frac{1}{2}$	CUP CHOPPED CELERY
$\frac{1}{4}$	CUP CHOPPED PECANS
2	TABLESPOONS SWEET PICKLE RELISH
2	TABLESPOONS DILL PICKLE RELISH
1	TEASPOON SALT
1	TEASPOON PEPPER

Chop the cooked chicken. In a large bowl mix the chicken, mayonnaise, mustard, celery, pecans, sweet pickle relish, dill pickle relish, salt, and pepper. Cover and chill for 4 hours. Serve over lettuce or stuff in summer tomatoes.

CUCUMBER SALAD

MAKES 8 SERVINGS

3	PEELED AND SLICED CUCUMBERS
1	LARGE ONION, PEELED AND SLICED INTO RINGS
1	LARGE GREEN PEPPER, SLICED LENGTHWISE
2	LARGE RIPE TOMATOES, QUARTERED
$\frac{1}{2}$	CUP VINEGAR
$\frac{1}{2}$	CUP WATER
1	TABLESPOON OLIVE OIL
$\frac{1}{4}$	CUP ITALIAN DRESSING

In a large bowl combine the cucumbers, onion, green pepper, tomatoes, vinegar, water, olive oil, and Italian dressing. Mix well and chill for 1 hour before serving.

PASTA SALAD

MAKES 8 SERVINGS

1	POUND PASTA (ANY STYLE)
1	DICED GREEN BELL PEPPER
1	DICED RED BELL PEPPER
1	DICED RED ONION
1	(10-OUNCE) BAG FROZEN GREEN PEAS
1	(12-OUNCE) BOTTLE ITALIAN SALAD DRESSING
½	CUP GRATED PARMESAN CHEESE

Cook the pasta in boiling, salted water until tender. Drain and rinse in cold water. Combine the pasta, green pepper, red pepper, onion, peas, and salad dressing in a large bowl. Mix well, being careful not to break the pasta. Cover and refrigerate for 2 to 3 hours to let the flavors come together. Toss again and add the cheese just before serving.

POTATO SALAD

MAKES 12 SERVINGS

3	TABLESPOONS SUGAR
3	TABLESPOONS APPLE CIDER VINEGAR
1	LARGE RED ONION, FINELY CHOPPED
2	POUNDS NEW POTATOES, QUARTERED
$\frac{3}{4}$	CUP MAYONNAISE
$\frac{1}{4}$	CUP MUSTARD
2	TEASPOONS CELERY SEED
1	TABLESPOON SALT
1	TEASPOON BLACK PEPPER
1	POUND BACON, COOKED CRISP AND CRUMBLED

In a large bowl mix together the sugar and vinegar. Add the onion and set aside. Cover the potatoes with water in a large pot over high heat and boil until they can be easily pierced with a fork, about 10 minutes. Be careful not to overcook them. Drain and rinse with cold water. Add the mayonnaise, mustard, and celery seed to the onion mixture and mix well. Add the potatoes and toss until well coated. Season to taste with the salt and pepper. Sprinkle the bacon over the potato salad and serve.

RED BEAN SALAD

MAKES 2 SERVINGS

1	(15-OUNCE) CAN RED KIDNEY BEANS, DRAINED
2	HARD-BOILED EGGS, CHOPPED
6	SWEET PICKLES, CHOPPED
¼	CUP MAYONNAISE
	SALT AND PEPPER

In a mixing bowl combine the beans, eggs, pickles, and mayonnaise. Cover and refrigerate until ready to serve. Before serving add salt and pepper to taste.

Loretta at Tootsie's in Nashville in the 1960s.

GLORIA LAND

In the summer of 1967, my career had really taken off. I had just had the twins, along with the four older kids.

Doo and I were running around like chickens with their heads cut off trying to record, do the Wilburn Brothers TV show, and perform shows. It was crazy, and to top it off, trying to find someone to watch the kids for us was almost impossible. Both Doo's mom and my mom came and tried to help as much as they could, but it had gotten to where if we were going to really do this singing career, we had to have a full-time nanny.

You know how when you're at your wits' end and God just seems to lend you a helping hand? Well, for me the answer to my prayers came in the form of a twenty-eight-year-old woman from Brinkley, Arkansas. Gloria Land is her name, and she is still with me today. Gloria came to live with us when the twins were just a year old. I used to tell her she had to be the bravest woman I know to take on six kids . . . someone else's six kids.

It was hard for me at first watchin' someone caring for my babies and my home. I have to admit that there was times I felt unneeded, but I will tell you—and Gloria, if you read this—there is no way I could have ever gotten anywhere in this business without her. Knowing your babies are safe, fed, and loved means everything to you when you're away.

As the years went by, Gloria and I became like sisters. When I would come home, she would kind of stand back and let me do the mothering. Most of the time when I came home off the road, we would both do the cooking. Gloria is a great cook.

In the summer, she and I would do all the canning and things. Even to this day, holidays have always been a mixture of Gloria's and my cooking. I make the chicken and dumplins and the green beans. Gloria makes her angel yeast biscuits and the greatest fruit salad you have ever eaten.

I have to laugh when I say Gloria and I are kinda like them Baldwin sisters that were on *The Waltons* TV show. I love her so much, and she will never know how beholden I am to her for all she has done for my family and me.

Gloria and me will be sisters forever.

64

CARROT & RAISIN SALAD

MAKES 12 SERVINGS

4	CUPS GRATED CARROTS
$\frac{1}{2}$	CUP RAISINS
$1\frac{1}{2}$	CUPS GRATED APPLE
1	(10-OUNCE) CAN SLICED MARASCHINO CHERRIES, DRAINED
$\frac{1}{2}$	TEASPOON LEMON JUICE
3	TEASPOONS SUGAR
2	TABLESPOONS SALAD DRESSING (MIRACLE WHIP)
2 to 3	TEASPOONS MILK

In a large bowl, toss the carrots, raisins, apple, and cherries together. Add the lemon juice, sugar, salad dressing, and milk. Mix well and serve.

Gloria Land in the late 1990s.

MUSTARD PICKLES

MAKES 12 PINTS

1	GALLON (16 CUPS) WATER
$\frac{1}{2}$	CUP PLUS 1 TABLESPOON SALT
15	FRESH CUCUMBERS
$\frac{1}{2}$	GALLON (8 CUPS) CIDER VINEGAR
1	CUP SUGAR
$\frac{1}{2}$	CUP PREPARED MUSTARD

Combine the water and ½ cup of the salt in a large bowl. Soak the cucumbers in the refrigerator for 8 to 10 hours or overnight, making sure they are covered with water. Drain the cucumbers. In a large bowl combine the cider vinegar, sugar, mustard, and the remaining 1 tablespoon salt. Pour over the cucumbers. Cover completely. The pickles will keep for years in open jar or a crock.

BEET RELISH

MAKES 1 CUP

2	CUPS COARSELY CHOPPED COOKED BEETS
1	TABLESPOON CHOPPED RED ONION
2	TABLESPOONS RED WINE VINEGAR
1	TEASPOON SUGAR
2	TABLESPOONS DIJON MUSTARD
3	TABLESPOONS VEGETABLE OIL
	SALT AND PEPPER

In a large bowl combine the beets, onion, vinegar, sugar, mustard, oil, and salt and pepper to taste. Mix well. Cover and store in the refrigerator until chilled.

Loretta as a teenager in the 1940s.

CUCUMBER RELISH

MAKES 2 QUARTS

8	QUARTS PEELED AND GRATED CUCUMBERS, ABOUT 20
1	CUP SALT
12	SMALL DRIED ONIONS
2	SWEET PEPPERS, DICED
6	MEDIUM CARROTS, GRATED
1	TEASPOON MUSTARD SEEDS
2	TEASPOONS TURMERIC
12	WHOLE CLOVES
7	CUPS SUGAR
1	QUART (4 CUPS) VINEGAR

In a large bowl mix the cucumbers and salt. Refrigerate, covered, 8 to 10 hours or overnight. Drain the cucumbers and discard the juice. Transfer the cucumbers to a large saucepan. Add the onions, sweet peppers, and carrots to the cucumbers. Stir in the mustard seeds, turmeric, cloves, sugar, and vinegar. Boil for 5 minutes. Remove from the heat. Ladle into sterilized pint jars, leaving ½ inch of headspace. Seal with 2-piece lids and process in a boiling water bath for 10 minutes.

★ BREADS ★

OLD-FASHIONED IRON SKILLET CORNBREAD

MEXICAN CORNBREAD

SPOON BREAD

CORN LIGHT BREAD

YEAST BREAD

ZUCCHINI BREAD

HOMEMADE CRACKERS

OLD-FASHIONED IRON SKILLET CORNBREAD

MAKES 8 SERVINGS

When me and Doo got married, I got two wedding gifts. One was a little cotton nightgown Doo's mom gave me, and the other was a big old iron skillet my mommy gave to me. Do you know to this day I still have that old cast-iron skillet and use it. I tell everybody the best and the only way to make my cornbread is in an iron skillet. If you ain't got one, go buy one. You don't know what you're missin'. I love pies and cakes—don't get me wrong. But over all the sweets in the world, I would much rather have a tall glass of milk with a big old piece of cornbread crumbled inside. Just give me a spoon and I'm in heaven.

½	CUP VEGETABLE OIL
2	CUPS SELF-RISING CORNMEAL
2	EGGS
1½	CUPS BUTTERMILK OR SWEET MILK

Preheat the oven to 350°. Pour the oil in an iron skillet. Heat the skillet in the oven. In a medium bowl mix the cornmeal, eggs, and buttermilk together. Remove the hot skillet from the oven. Increase the temperature to 400°. Pour a little of the hot oil into the batter and stir. Pour the batter into the skillet. Bake for 15 to 20 minutes or until golden and crispy. Serve hot with lots of butter.

NOTE: IF YOUR IRON SKILLET IS NEW, YOU WILL NEED TO CURE IT BY OILING AND BAKING IT IN YOUR OVEN SEVERAL TIMES ON ABOUT 200° BEFORE USING. REMEMBER NEVER TO USE DISH SOAP ON YOUR SKILLET. JUST WIPE IT CLEAN.

MEXICAN CORNBREAD

MAKES 8 SERVINGS

$\frac{1}{2}$	CUP VEGETABLE OIL
2	CUPS SELF-RISING CORNMEAL
2	EGGS
$1\frac{1}{2}$	CUPS BUTTERMILK OR SWEET MILK
1	JALAPEÑO PEPPER, CHOPPED (ADD MORE IF YOU'RE FEELING SPICY)
1	(15-OUNCE) CAN CREAM STYLE CORN
1	MEDIUM YELLOW ONION, CHOPPED
4	FRESH GREEN ONIONS, CHOPPED
1	CUP SHREDDED SHARP CHEDDAR CHEESE
1	TEASPOON SALT

Preheat the oven to 350°. Pour the oil in an iron skillet. Heat the skillet in the oven while mixing the batter. In a medium bowl, mix the cornmeal, eggs, buttermilk, jalapeño, cream style corn, yellow onion, green onions, cheese, and salt together. Remove the hot skillet from the oven. Increase the oven temperature to 400°. Pour a little of the hot oil into the batter and stir. Pour the cornbread batter into the skillet. Bake for 15 to 20 minutes or until golden and crispy. Serve hot with lots of butter.

NOTE: TO SPICE IT UP, YOU CAN ADD SOME GREEN CHILIES.

SPOON BREAD

MAKES 8 SERVINGS

2	CUPS WATER
1	CUP YELLOW CORNMEAL
4	TABLESPOONS BUTTER
1	TEASPOON SALT
4	EGGS, BEATEN
1	CUP MILK

Preheat the oven to 375°. In a medium saucepan over high heat bring the water to a boil. Add the cornmeal and stir until the mixture is thick and creamy. Remove from the heat. Add the butter and salt and allow the mixture to cool a bit. Mix in the eggs and milk. Pour the mixture into a greased casserole dish and bake in the oven for 20 minutes or until golden brown. Use a spoon to serve while it's hot.

COOKING FOR CELEBRITIES

When we first come to Nashville, Doo and I got a room with a little tiny kitchenette. Who would show up to eat? George Jones. He was in the same motel, and he was figuring on me cooking. He come in early in the morning. He never went to bed. This is why he showed up so early.

Patsy Cline loved my cooking. She'd come eat it just about every day. Dottie West would come. Dottie liked roasts. She liked steaks and chicken. It didn't matter to Dottie. She'd eat anything, as long as it was cooked. Patsy was the same way, but Patsy loved rabbit or squirrel. If you fried a rabbit and didn't call her and she found out, she wouldn't speak to you for a week.

Conway Twitty liked beans. He liked fried potatoes. He liked cornbread. He *loved* cornbread. He liked chicken and dumplins, too. Conway was easy to please, because he loved to eat.

Conway had this jet, you know. He took me on that jet once, and I was scared to death. I prayed the whole time we went up and the whole time we was in the air. He said, "You go with me one time, and you'll sell them buses." Who wound up getting another bus? Conway did. He eventually told me, "You're right, Loretta. I'll never go on a plane no more. Buses for me."

Tammy Wynette loved to eat, too. Me and Tammy cooked for each other a bunch. She and George Richey come over to Hawaii and spent two or three weeks with me once. Well, one morning, they got up—I think it was about three o'clock in the morning. We heard them giggling and laughing and carrying on. I said, "Doo, what in the world's funny in there?" He didn't know, so we got up and went in the kitchen. They were in there cooking. They were making biscuits, gravy, eggs, bacon. They had the whole works. And they had grits. I never did get used to grits, but they liked them.

When the movie was going on, I cooked for Sissy Spacek and Tommy Lee Jones. Whatever I was cooking, they'd come in the kitchen and eat. It wasn't no big thing because we were together for a year.

At first, Doo was jealous of Tommy Lee. Tommy Lee comes to meet Doolittle. He's got his hair crew cut, just like Doo had. And he's dyed it red because Doo has red hair. He has a sweater just like Doolittle had when we got married. I don't know where he got a picture of Doo's sweater, but he found one somewhere. He come in with that sweater on, his hair dyed red, and that crew cut. And Doo wouldn't have nothing to do with him. He wouldn't even speak to him. I said, "Doo, this is Tommy Lee." He said, "Yeah," and he just kept watching the TV. Tommy Lee said, "Well, how do you like my hair, Man?" "Yeah." This is how he answered him. 'Til right in the middle of the movie, then he got to really loving Tommy Lee.

I guess I've cooked for nearly everybody that's been part of my life. The celebrities haven't been all that much different than anybody else. At least not the one's that's been around me.

Doo and Loretta with Sissy Spacek and Tommy Lee Jones in 1980.

CORN LIGHT BREAD

MAKES 8 SERVINGS

1	EGG
½	CUP SUGAR
1½	CUPS BUTTERMILK
½	CUP ALL-PURPOSE FLOUR
1	TEASPOON SALT
1	TEASPOON BAKING SODA
2	CUPS YELLOW CORNMEAL

Preheat the oven to 350°. In a bowl beat the egg and add the sugar and buttermilk. In a separate bowl sift together the flour, salt, baking soda, and cornmeal. Add the sifted dry ingredients to the egg mixture and mix well. Pour into a buttered loaf pan and bake for 20 to 25 minutes until golden brown.

BREAD

Loretta made this loaf in her kitchen.

It's hard for me to follow a recipe if I don't know it. I cook like Mommy. She'd taste whatever she was cooking until everything was okay.

When I got one of those bread makers, I really wasn't too sure of myself, because I had always made my bread by hand. But now I've got three bread makers, right? Because you never know what kids are coming in or who they'll bring with them. They'll come in, and they'll want a loaf of bread or something.

The first two or three times I made bread with the bread makers, it turned out harder than a doggone rock. If you hit somebody over the head with it, it'd kill them. I just laid it in the window, out in the room where all the windows are. I said, I'm going to keep this bread, and I'm going to paint that stuff. I'm going to put a picture on it and paint it and say, "That's my bread, take it or leave it."

YEAST BREAD

MAKES 2 LOAVES

5½ to 6	CUPS ALL-PURPOSE FLOUR
2	PACKAGES DRY YEAST
3	TABLESPOONS SUGAR
1	TEASPOON SALT
2	CUPS WARM WATER
¼	CUP VEGETABLE OIL

In a bowl measure 2 cups of the flour. Add the yeast, sugar, and salt. Mix well. Add the water and oil. Beat until smooth. Add 1 more cup of the flour and mix well. Stir in more flour, enough to make a soft dough. Turn onto a floured surface and knead until smooth and elastic, 8 to 10 minutes. Place in a greased bowl, turning to grease all the dough. Cover and let rise in a warm place until doubled in size, about 1 hour. Punch down the dough, divide it in half, cover, and let it rest for 10 minutes. Shape into loaves. Place the loaves into greased 8½ x 4½-inch pans. Let rise in a warm place until doubled in size, about 1 hour. Preheat the oven to 400°. Bake for 30 to 35 minutes or until golden brown.

ZUCCHINI BREAD

MAKES 2 LOAVES

3	EGGS
1	CUP BROWN SUGAR
1	CUP GRANULATED SUGAR
1	CUP OIL
2	ZUCCHINIS, GRATED
1	TEASPOON VANILLA EXTRACT
3	CUPS ALL-PURPOSE FLOUR
½	TEASPOON GROUND CINNAMON
1	TEASPOON BAKING POWDER
1	TEASPOON BAKING SODA
1	TEASPOON SALT
1	CUP CHOPPED NUTS

Preheat the oven to 325°. Beat the eggs until fluffy. Stir in the brown sugar, granulated sugar, oil, zucchinis, and vanilla. In a separate bowl combine the flour, cinnamon, baking powder, baking soda, and salt. Stir in the zucchini mixture until well mixed. Stir in the nuts. Pour into two well-greased 9 x 5-inch loaf pans. Bake for 1 hour. Cool 10 minutes before removing from the pan. Cool thoroughly before slicing.

HOMEMADE CRACKERS

MAKES 4 DOZEN

3	CUPS UNCOOKED OATMEAL
2	CUPS UNBLEACHED FLOUR PLUS SOME FOR DUSTING
1	CUP WHEAT GERM
1	CUP WATER
3	TABLESPOONS SUGAR
1	TEASPOON SALT PLUS SOME FOR DUSTING
$\frac{3}{4}$	CUP VEGETABLE OIL

Preheat the oven to 350°. In a large bowl combine the oatmeal, flour, wheat germ, water, sugar, salt, and oil and mix well. Roll out the dough onto two lightly floured baking sheets. Sprinkle with salt. Lightly mark the dough into 1-inch squares with a butter knife. Be careful not to cut through the dough. Bake for 30 minutes or until crisp. Watch edges so they don't burn. Cut into squares before serving.

★ SIDE DISHES ★

BAKED POTATO WEDGES (TATER LOGS)
STUFFED BAKED POTATOES
TATER CAKES
HOMESTYLE FRIES
SCALLOPED POTATOES
LORETTA'S MASHED POTATOES
POTATO BALLS WITH SAUCE
POTATO ROLLS
COUNTRY FRIED CABBAGE
COUNTRY FRIED CREAM CORN
COUNTRY FRIED OKRA
FRIED APPLES
FRIED CORN
COLESLAW
CORN FRITTERS WITH YELLOW PEPPER SALSA
MARINATED VEGETABLES
MARINATED ASPARAGUS
HONEY GLAZED CARROTS
PINTO BEANS & RICE
STEWED CABBAGE
STUFFED CABBAGE LEAVES
SWEET POTATO CASSEROLE
CORN CASSEROLE
SQUASH CASSEROLE
EGGPLANT CASSEROLE
ZUCCHINI CASSEROLE
DEVILISH DEVILED EGGS
SOUTHERN GREEN BEANS & NEW POTATOES
HUSH PUPPIES
TURNIP GREENS
WHITE BEANS
PATCHWORK QUILT RICE
MACARONI WITH CHEESE
TOMATO PIE

BAKED POTATO WEDGES (TATER LOGS)

MAKES 8 SERVINGS

4	LARGE BAKING POTATOES, QUARTERED LENGTHWISE
¼	CUP OIL
1	TABLESPOON GARLIC POWDER
2	TEASPOONS SEASONED SALT
1	TEASPOON PEPPER

Preheat the oven to 400°. In a large bowl toss the potatoes with the oil to coat. Sprinkle with the garlic powder, seasoned salt, and pepper. Toss again to coat well. Place on a baking sheet and bake until crispy on the outside and tender on the inside, about 1 hour. Remove the potatoes from the oven and lightly salt again. Serve hot.

STUFFED BAKED POTATOES

MAKES 8 SERVINGS

4	LARGE BAKING POTATOES
$\frac{1}{2}$	STICK BUTTER
$\frac{1}{2}$	CUP MILK
2	GARLIC CLOVES, FINELY MINCED
4	OUNCES CRUMBLED BLUE CHEESE
	SALT AND PEPPER
4	SLICES BACON, COOKED CRISP AND CRUMBLED

Preheat the oven to 400°. Pierce the potatoes several times with a fork. Wrap in foil and bake for 1 hour and 30 minutes, or until tender. Unwrap the potatoes and slice in half lengthwise. Reduce the oven temperature to 350°. Scoop out the inside and put into a medium mixing bowl. Add the butter, milk, garlic, blue cheese, and salt and pepper to taste. Beat until smooth. You want this mixture to be like mashed potatoes. Spoon the mixture back into the potato shells and top with the bacon. Bake for 20 minutes. Serve hot.

TATER CAKES

MAKES 10 SERVINGS

5	CUPS CREAMED POTATOES
1	EGG, BEATEN
1	TABLESPOON FLOUR
	SALT AND PEPPER
	VEGETABLE OIL FOR FRYING

In a large bowl mix together the creamed potatoes, egg, flour, and salt and pepper to taste. Shape the mixture into patties. Heat 2 to 3 inches of oil in a cast-iron skillet over medium-high heat and fry the patties for about 1 minute on each side, or until brown. Serve hot.

Loretta and Doo in the 1980s.

THE LYNNS AT MEALTIME

When I was a young girl at home, when we went to the table everything was quiet. Nobody cut up; nobody did anything. There was no problems talked over. Everything was, "Please pass this," as it went around.

There was ten kids in Doo's family. They went to the table talking about the whole world's problems. When I married into that family, it was absolutely from daylight to dark. I'm telling you, I couldn't eat.

I went around to see Mommy, and Mommy says, "Loretty, what's happened to you? You're as skinny as you can be!" I said, "Mommy, I can't eat." She asked why, and I said, "They're noisy at the table." But that's where they fought all their battles, right there at the table, with biscuits flying through the air.

When Doo and I first started having kids, mealtimes were like they had been with my family. We just passed the plate around, and we'd be very nice about it. We didn't make no big deals out of anything. If Doo had anything to tell me about the work that day, he'd tell me. But we didn't bring up a lot of stuff at the table. We always felt that the table was not the place to go through the fighting and the carrying on. So it was very relaxed.

Doo might ask me how my day was, but if I started, he'd say, "Ah, forget it. I'm sorry I asked." I was the one that moaned and groaned about things. But I was the one that was holding down two jobs, too. I'd rush home and get the house cleaned up and get supper for him before he got home. That was after working at the neighbor's. That's how I paid the rent, cooking every day for them.

When I started singing, coming home to mealtimes bothered me so bad. I'd come home to an absolutely wild house. We'd go to the table, and Patsy and Peggy made more noise than all the first four kids did. Doo would say, "Tell me, girls, how did things go today at school?" Well, you might as well have opened up the Bible and started preaching. Because something happened to one of them and the other one it didn't, and they'd talk backwards and forwards.

Doo always sat at the end of the table. He had Peggy sitting on his left side, and Patsy sat on his right. When I come home, Peggy would have to move. But she didn't want me sitting next to Doo; I wasn't allowed to. Sometimes she won that argument, and sometimes she didn't. But if Peggy won, then she was on my right side, and she was left-handed. And every time I'd start to my mouth with a forkful of something, Peggy'd come up with her elbow and knock it all over the place. But that was where they set, and it was quite a deal when I got home.

We always had dinner at six o'clock. We all sat around the table and held hands for the prayer. At first, our second daughter, Cissie, would always say this little prayer for the meal:

> God is great,
> God is good,
> Let us thank Him for the food.
> By his name
> It must be said,
> Give us, God, our daily bread. Amen.

Then, when the twins come along, they always said the prayer. That was the first thing that happened at the table. No matter how hungry anybody was, they didn't dare make a move 'til the prayer was done. If they did, they'd get smacked, probably. I certainly didn't want to make that first move.

But after the babies came along, when I'd come home, it was hard for me to eat with them because of all the ruckus that was going on around the table. Me and my first kids was taught not to be like that. When the babies come along and I wasn't home all the time, Doolittle'd come to the table, and he'd hit that table and say, "Okay, girls, tell your dad what happened at school today." They'd go on and on. And the more Peggy Jean got on, the bigger it got. I'd look at Doo and say, "Doo, she's lying. Why are you eggin' her on? Don't be asking her anymore." But they'd laugh at her, so the more she'd tell, the bigger it got. And you never knew when it ended and when it started.

There was one thing about dinner that Patsy and Peggy liked when I came home. When I wasn't home, Doo made them do the dishes. When I came home, I did them. I'd tell Doo, "Doolittle, them girls are too little to be standing up there at the sink." They liked that.

87

HOMESTYLE FRIES

MAKES 5 SERVINGS

$1\frac{1}{2}$	POUNDS BAKING POTATOES, NOT PEELED
$\frac{1}{2}$	TEASPOON PAPRIKA
$\frac{1}{4}$	TEASPOON GARLIC POWDER
$\frac{1}{2}$	TEASPOON ONION POWDER
$\frac{1}{4}$	TEASPOON SALT
$\frac{1}{4}$	TEASPOON BLACK PEPPER
	VEGETABLE COOKING SPRAY

Preheat the oven to 425°. Cut the potatoes into ¼-inch slices and pat dry with paper towels. Combine the paprika, garlic powder, onion powder, salt, and pepper in a large sealable plastic bag. Add the potatoes and shake well to coat. Arrange the potatoes in a single layer on a baking sheet coated with cooking spray. Bake for 20 minutes. Serve hot.

SCALLOPED POTATOES

MAKES 8 SERVINGS

6 to 8	THINLY SLICED POTATOES
3	CUPS SHREDDED CHEDDAR CHEESE
1	TABLESPOON ALL-PURPOSE FLOUR
	SALT AND PEPPER
2½	CUPS MILK
1	TABLESPOON BUTTER, CUT INTO SMALL PIECES

Preheat the oven to 400°. Soak the potatoes in cold water for 30 minutes. Drain and pat dry. In a buttered casserole dish, alternate layers of the potatoes and cheese until all the ingredients are used. Sprinkle the flour and salt and pepper to taste over each layer. Pour the milk over the casserole and dot the top with the butter. Bake until golden brown and the potatoes are tender, about 45 minutes.

LORETTA'S MASHED POTATOES

MAKES 8 SERVINGS

*I know y'all are thinking, "mashed potatoes?" But you would be surprised
how many folks can't make good mashed potatoes. For those of you who
do, skip this recipe. For those of you who ain't quite sure, follow along.*

6	WASHED AND PEELED MEDIUM RED POTATOES (I LIKE TO LEAVE THE SKIN ON ABOUT 2 OR 3 AND PEEL THE REST)
1	(4-OUNCE) CAN EVAPORATED MILK
1	LARGE TABLESPOON BUTTER
	SALT AND PEPPER

Cut the potatoes into chunks. In a medium saucepan, combine the potatoes with enough water to cover. Cook over medium heat until tender, about 20 minutes. Drain and place in a large mixing bowl. Add the evaporated milk and butter. Using a hand mixer, mix the potatoes on low to medium speed (depending on how whipped you like your mashed potatoes). Add salt and pepper to taste.

POTATO BALLS WITH SAUCE

MAKES 6 SERVINGS

POTATO BALLS

6	MEDIUM POTATOES
1	MEDIUM ONION, MINCED
1	(4-OUNCE) CAN RIPE OLIVES, CHOPPED
1	PLUS 1 EGG
	DASH OF ONION SALT
	DASH OF GARLIC SALT
	CRACKER MEAL

SAUCE

8	OUNCES CHEDDAR CHEESE, GRATED
$\frac{1}{2}$	CUP SOUR CREAM
2	TABLESPOONS CHOPPED GREEN ONIONS
4	TABLESPOONS BUTTER, SOFTENED

Peel and cube the potatoes. In a saucepan over high heat cook the potatoes in boiling water for about 12 minutes or until soft. Mash the potatoes. Add the onion, olives, 1 of the eggs, onion salt, and garlic salt. Let the mixture cool. Form into balls $1\frac{1}{2}$ inches in diameter. Beat the remaining egg. Dip the balls into the beaten egg and roll in the cracker meal. Refrigerate 8 to 10 hours or overnight.

For the sauce, combine the cheese, sour cream, green onions, and butter. Mix well. Heat $\frac{3}{4}$ inch of oil in a skillet over high heat. Fry the balls for about 5 minutes or until golden brown. Serve hot with the sauce.

POTATO ROLLS

MAKES 12 ROLLS

1	CUP SCALDED MILK
1	CUP HOT MASHED POTATOES
$\frac{1}{2}$	CUP SHORTENING
$\frac{1}{4}$	CUP SUGAR
2	TEASPOONS SALT
1	PACKAGE YEAST
$\frac{1}{2}$	CUP WARM WATER
2	EGGS, BEATEN
$1\frac{1}{2}$	PLUS $3\frac{1}{2}$ CUPS ALL-PURPOSE FLOUR

Preheat the oven to 425°. Combine the milk, potatoes, shortening, sugar, and salt in a bowl. Let stand until lukewarm. Dissolve the yeast in the warm water. Add the eggs to the yeast and pour into the potato mixture. Mix well. Add $1\frac{1}{2}$ cups of the flour and beat well. Cover and let stand in a warm place until full of bubbles. Stir in the remaining $3\frac{1}{2}$ cups flour to make dough fairly stiff. Knead on a floured surface until smooth. Return to a greased bowl, cover, and chill in the refrigerator for 30 minutes. When chilled shape the dough and place on a greased pan. Let it rise until doubled. Bake for 15 to 20 minutes.

COUNTRY FRIED CABBAGE

MAKES 4 SERVINGS

*This is one of my favorite country side dishes. I love this served
with my good old baked pork chops, black-eyed peas, fried potatoes and
onions, and a side of fresh coleslaw. Hey, that's what I call eating.*

5	STRIPS BACON
1	MEDIUM HEAD CABBAGE, SLICED INTO LARGE PIECES
1	SMALL YELLOW ONION, CHOPPED
	SALT AND PEPPER

Fry the bacon in a skillet over medium-high heat until crisp. Remove the bacon, reserving the drippings. Drain the bacon on paper towels. Add the cabbage and onions to the skillet. Season with the salt and pepper to taste. Cover the skillet and cook over medium heat, stirring occasionally. When the cabbage is tender, crumble in the bacon. Mix well and serve immediately.

COUNTRY FRIED CREAM CORN

MAKES 6 TO 8 SERVINGS

4 to 5	EARS CORN
3 to 4	STRIPS BACON
3	TABLESPOONS FLOUR
$\frac{2}{3}$	CUP SWEET MILK
	SALT AND PEPPER

Remove 3 cups of corn from the cob. Place the corn in a medium skillet. It's best to cook in an iron skillet if you have one. If not, any medium skillet will do. Add enough water to cover the corn. Cook over medium heat, covered with a lid. Boil the corn until tender, about 7 minutes. Cut the strips of bacon into 2-inch pieces. In another skillet, fry the bacon until crisp. Remove the bacon from the skillet and drain on paper towels. Reserve the drippings.

Combine the flour and sweet milk in a pint jar. Place a lid on the jar and shake until all the bubbles are gone and the flour and milk are well mixed. Pour the flour mixture over the cooked corn. Add the bacon drippings and salt and pepper to taste. Cover and cook over low heat until thickened. Add the bacon and stir. And there you have it, my Country Fried Cream Corn.

VARIATION: YOU CAN USE CANNED OR FROZEN CORN, BUT IT JUST AIN'T AS GOOD.

CREAM CORN

I come home off the road. Doo was drinking those days, but I didn't know how much he was drinking. I got in about eight o'clock that night and waited for Doo. He come in about nine o'clock, and I was still up because I was waiting for him to come in. His meal was sitting on the stove, so we both sat down at the kitchen table.

Doo looked over at me and said, "Eat!" I said, "Honey, we just had a steak awhile ago. I'm really full." Doo always told me, "Loretta, you're getting too thin. Eat before you come home." So that's what I had done. All of us had stopped the bus, gotten out, and eaten a big steak just before we got into Nashville. So when I got home, I wasn't hungry.

And a few minutes later, he said it again, "Eat!" I said, "Honey, I'm not hungry." Now, our housekeeper, Gloria Land, had set a glass of milk out in front of me and said, "Well, maybe you can drink a glass of milk." Doo picked that great big glass of milk up and poured it over my head. I looked across that table and saw the steam coming off a big bowl of country fried cream corn, and I thought, "Buddy, you've had it." I picked that corn up and just put it on top of his head.

The corn had a little bit of stiffener in it, like flour and milk—well, that's what got him. It went all over his head. It dried on his face, and he looked like someone from the Addams Family. It had his hair sticking straight up in different places. I'm telling you it was the awfulest looking thing I ever seen. He didn't take a bath for three days. Oh, he wanted everybody on the ranch to see what his wife had done to him. Three days he slept on the couch, and then I had to leave. He didn't talk to me the whole time I was home. I imagine he took a bath the minute I left.

COUNTRY FRIED OKRA

MAKES 4 SERVINGS

Winter, summer, spring, or fall there ain't nothing I love better than fresh country okra. My vegetable garden wouldn't be complete without plenty of homegrown okra. Remember to always select the small, tender pods even when buying them at the grocery store. Most people either buy or pick too much okra or not enough. The best way I've found to figure out how much you need is four pods per person.

1	POUND FRESH, TENDER OKRA
1	CUP ALL-PURPOSE FLOUR
1	CUP CORNMEAL
	SALT AND PEPPER
1 to 2	CUPS SWEET MILK
	VEGETABLE OIL FOR FRYING

Wash the okra and cut into ½-inch pieces. Throw away the stem ends. In a paper or plastic bag, combine the flour, cornmeal, and salt and pepper to taste. Pour the sweet milk into a medium bowl. Dip the okra in the milk several times. Do not let it sit in the milk or the okra will soak up too much milk. Place the okra in the bag with the dry mixture and get to shakin' until the okra is well coated. Pour the oil into a frying pan about half full and heat to 375°. Fry the okra in the hot oil until brown and crispy, about 3 minutes. Drain on paper towels before serving.

FRIED APPLES

MAKES 8 SERVINGS

1	STICK BUTTER
4	LARGE APPLES, PEELED, CORED, AND DICED
½	CUP GRANULATED SUGAR
½	CUP FIRMLY PACKED BROWN SUGAR
1	TEASPOON GROUND CINNAMON
	PINCH OF SALT

Melt the butter in a cast-iron skillet over medium heat. Add the apples, granulated sugar, brown sugar, cinnamon, and salt. Cover and cook for about 12 minutes. Uncover and cook for about 15 minutes longer or until the apples are tender.

Loretta's parents, Clara and Ted Webb in the 1940s.

FRIED CORN

MAKES 16 SERVINGS

10	EARS CORN
1	STICK BUTTER
½	CUP MILK
2	TABLESPOONS SUGAR
1	TABLESPOON FLOUR
	SALT AND PEPPER

Remove the corn kernels from the cobs with a sharp knife. Melt the butter in a cast-iron skillet over medium heat. Add the corn and cook for about 10 minutes. Add the milk and sugar and continue to cook for an additional 5 minutes. Stir in the flour and salt and pepper to taste. Cook until thick and golden, adding more milk if necessary. Serve hot.

COLESLAW

MAKES 10 SERVINGS

1	HEAD WHITE CABBAGE
1	HEAD RED CABBAGE
$\frac{3}{4}$	CUP MAYONNAISE
1	TABLESPOON SUGAR
1	TABLESPOON APPLE CIDER VINEGAR
2	TEASPOONS CELERY SEED
	SALT AND PEPPER

Grate the white and red cabbages. Mix together in a large bowl. Set the cabbage aside. In a small bowl combine the mayonnaise, sugar, vinegar, and celery seed. Add to the cabbage and mix well. Season with salt and pepper to taste. Cover tightly and place in the refrigerator for 4 hours before serving.

CORN FRITTERS WITH YELLOW PEPPER SALSA

MAKES 12 SERVINGS

YELLOW PEPPER SALSA

1	TABLESPOON VEGETABLE OIL
1	SMALL ONION, CHOPPED
1	MEDIUM YELLOW BELL PEPPER, CHOPPED
2 to 3	PICKLED JALAPEÑO PEPPERS, MINCED
1	(10-OUNCE) JAR APPLE JELLY
4	TEASPOONS CORNSTARCH
2	TABLESPOONS WATER

CORN FRITTERS

$\frac{1}{2}$	CUP ALL-PURPOSE FLOUR
$\frac{1}{2}$	CUP YELLOW CORNMEAL
$1\frac{1}{2}$	TEASPOONS BAKING POWDER
2	TEASPOONS SUGAR
$\frac{1}{2}$	TEASPOON SALT
3	LARGE EGGS
$\frac{2}{3}$	CUP MILK
$\frac{1}{4}$	CUP MELTED BUTTER
1	(1-POUND) CAN WHOLE KERNEL CORN, DRAINED
3	GREEN ONIONS, CHOPPED
2	TABLESPOONS VEGETABLE OIL
1	GREEN BELL PEPPER HALF (OPTIONAL FOR THE SALSA BOWL)

Prepare the salsa the day before serving. In a medium saucepan heat the vegetable oil over medium-high heat. Add the onion, yellow pepper, and jalapeño peppers. Sauté for 1 minute. Add the jelly and stir until melted. In a small bowl mix the cornstarch with the water. Add to the pepper mixture and cook, stirring until thick. Pour the salsa into a small bowl. Cover and refrigerate 8 to 10 hours or overnight.

For the corn fritters, in a large bowl mix the flour, cornmeal, baking powder, sugar, and salt. Set the mixture aside. In a medium bowl whisk the eggs with the milk, butter, corn, and green onions. Add the egg mixture to the flour mixture and mix until the dry ingredients are moistened. In a large skillet heat the vegetable oil over medium-high heat. Drop the fritter batter by tablespoons into the hot oil. Cook for 1 to 2 minutes on each side or until golden brown, adding more oil as needed. To serve, fill the green bell pepper half with the Yellow Pepper Salsa. Arrange the fritters on a platter with the salsa. Serve immediately.

MARINATED VEGETABLES

MAKES 8 SERVINGS

2	CUPS SALAD OIL
1	CUP RED WINE VINEGAR
2	TABLESPOONS SUGAR
2	TEASPOONS DRY MUSTARD
$\frac{1}{2}$	TEASPOON PEPPER
1	(12-OUNCE) BOTTLE ITALIAN DRESSING
1	PINT CHERRY TOMATOES
1	SMALL CAULIFLOWER HEAD
1	(16-OUNCE) CAN GREEN BEANS
1	(4-OUNCE) CAN RIPE PITTED OLIVES
1	RED ONION, SLICED
$\frac{1}{2}$	POUND FRESH MUSHROOMS, SLICED
1	GREEN PEPPER, SLICED

In a large container mix the salad oil, vinegar, sugar, dry mustard, pepper, and Italian dressing. In a large bowl mix the tomatoes, cauliflower, green beans, olives, red onion, mushrooms, and green pepper. Pour the dressing over the vegetables. Cover and refrigerate for 8 hours. Serve cold.

LORETTA LEARNS TO CAN

When I lived out in the state of Washington, I raised a garden. This lady, she said, "Let's cook and can some stuff for the fair." That was Edna Brann. Edna Brann wasn't that much older than me, maybe eight or nine years.

I didn't know that much about gardening. I just helped Mommy. Mommy would do the garden, and I'd just go behind her and drop the seeds or whatever. But this is something you do if you have to eat. I had four kids at the time, and I needed to feed them. I never had canned either. Mommy would have me washing the jars while she would be doing the canning.

Edna's daddy had rented us this little three-room house for thirty-five dollars a month. Her daddy lived on the place, too. He had this big garden spot, and he said I could use it. Well, Doolittle fixed it up. He tilled it and got it all ready for me. I had enough stuff in the garden for me and Edna, too.

I had put the garden out, and it was growing. I said, "I need to learn how to can, because I don't know how." Edna said, "Well, I'll learn you."

Edna showed me how to can. She told me how to put everything in the jars. She taught me everything about canning, and, by golly, it didn't take me long to pick it up. I took that canning and run with it. I canned everything I had in the garden, stuff that people wouldn't even think about canning: cabbages, potatoes, the whole thing. I would open them cans and just add the butter, the salt, or whatever.

The Northwest Washington District Fair came along, and Edna always took her stuff to the fair. I took all my stuff to the fair when she did. And you know who won? Me!

I think I cheated a little bit, but I didn't know. I wanted my canning to look pretty, not just good. I thought the way it looked would be how you would win, you know? When I made mustard greens, I placed it in the jar with the stem up. I placed the mustard leaves in the can, all the way up, all around the can. Then, when I canned the small potatoes and green beans, I placed them little potatoes with the green beans next to them, all around the quart jar. I took my vegetables out of the garden and placed them in paper plates. I paid a lot of attention to what I was doing. Everything that I fixed to take to the fair, I placed just perfect.

Somebody seen that I worked hard at that, and I won prizes over all of them. I won seventeen blue ribbons, eight red ribbons, and seven white ribbons. Isn't that something? For me, that was just like being Miss America. They had a picture of me blowed up at the fair, as big as the gate. I had jeans on and this old floppy shirt, and I was about three feet off the floor, jumping high.

I don't know if they gave me first prize because they felt sorry for me or not. Of course, they was all excited about me winning so much. When they seen the little place I was living in, they were happy I got it.

Edna never thought anything about me winning. She just knew my cans looked good, and they were still hot when I got them off the stove. And they were still hot when we got them to the fair, like seven miles away in Lynden.

I know all the women got mad at me. I was just fourteen years old, and it was my first year of canning. Here these women were, in their late forties and fifties. Edna said, "I won't come and teach you nothing else!" I think it made Edna a little mad. I think it hurt her feelings because she was the one that showed me how to can, and her canning didn't get nothing.

The man that let me have his garden let me use his jars. He let me do that for three summers. I thought that was great. When I took them back to him, I had them cleaned and took them back and put them right where he had them. I don't know what I would've done without him. But I bet you I left a thousand quarts of canned food in Washington when I left. That's always bothered me.

Not too long ago, I went out to the same little fair where I'd won all my ribbons. I started to call Edna up and tell everybody what she meant to me, and she fainted deader than a doornail. I don't know if it was the sun or what. I think she worked too hard to get things ready for that fair. I was worried sick, but her boy is a doctor, so he was with her. I was thankful for that.

I still raise a garden. I don't have to; I just like it. And I think the stuff you get out of the garden is better than you can get in the store. And I can because I think it's better than you can get in the cans at the store. The canned stuff, they chop that dadgum mustard up in little pieces. I don't do my mustard that way. I keep it whole. And I wash it, leaf by leaf, three times to make sure everything's off of it. I'd always rather have something homemade. If I make it myself, I know what it's supposed to taste like, and I know that I'm going to like it.

Loretta in Washington with her prize-winning canned goods.

105

MARINATED ASPARAGUS

MAKES 6 SERVINGS

1½	POUNDS FRESH ASPARAGUS
½	CUP PLUS 2 TABLESPOONS VIRGIN OLIVE OIL
1	TABLESPOON WHITE WINE VINEGAR
2	TABLESPOONS FRESH LEMON JUICE
	SALT AND PEPPER

Trim the asparagus. Add 2 tablespoons of the olive oil to a saucepan filled with water. Bring to a boil. Add the asparagus and cook for 2 minutes. Drain and rinse in ice cold water. Drain and arrange the asparagus in a 13 x 9-inch glass baking dish. In a small bowl mix the vinegar, lemon juice, salt and pepper to taste, and the remaining ½ cup olive oil, blending well with a whisk. Pour over the asparagus. Chill, covered, for at least 2 hours.

HONEY GLAZED CARROTS

MAKES 4 SERVINGS

3	TABLESPOONS HONEY
2	TABLESPOONS BUTTER
$\frac{1}{4}$	TEASPOON GRATED ORANGE RIND
1	TABLESPOON POPPY SEEDS
$\frac{1}{8}$	TEASPOON SALT
10 to 12	SMALL COOKED CARROTS

Combine the honey, butter, orange rind, poppy seeds, and salt together in a skillet over medium heat. Bring the mixture to a boil. Add the carrots and simmer for 10 to 12 minutes, turning frequently.

PINTO BEANS & RICE

MAKES 12 SERVINGS

1	(1-POUND) PACK SMOKED SAUSAGE
1	(16-OUNCE) BAG DRIED PINTO BEANS, SOAKED OVERNIGHT
	SALT AND PEPPER
2	CUPS UNCOOKED RICE (NOT MINUTE RICE)

Cut the sausage into ½-inch pieces. In a large pot combine the sausage, beans, and salt and pepper to taste. Add enough water to cover the beans. Bring the water to a full boil for 10 minutes. Reduce the heat to low, cover the pot, and simmer for 2 to 3 hours. Add water as needed. Cook the rice according to the instructions on the bag. Serve the rice topped with the beans and sausage.

COOKING ON THE BUS

I've got a whole kitchen on my bus. You know what I do in that kitchen? I pop popcorn most of the time. We've got everything in the kitchen to cook with, but who wants to dirty up the kitchen when I'm in bed? When I get through with a show at nighttime, it's time for bed, and that's the way it goes. There's not much cooking. It's hard to cook going down the highway. And my stove don't have hooks on it like the stoves on some buses do.

Once I was cooking beans, and I thought, "Surely to goodness the bus driver won't stop fast." I had them beans cooking on the back part of the stove, thinking they might slide a little but not that much. I heard something go clink, but I thought it was a dish in the sink. But when I looked back there, them beans was everywhere. They were all over the kitchen. They were in the bed. They were in the couch. They were in the chairs. We had beans everywhere, and we had to wait 'til we got to where we was going to clean them. Unless you've stopped, cooking on the road ain't no fun. It really ain't.

STEWED CABBAGE

MAKES 8 SERVINGS

1	LARGE CABBAGE, QUARTERED
$\frac{1}{4}$	POUND SMOKED BACON, CHOPPED
$\frac{1}{2}$	STICK BUTTER
1	TEASPOON SUGAR
1	TEASPOON RED PEPPER FLAKES
	SALT AND PEPPER

In a large saucepan combine the cabbage, bacon, butter, sugar, and red pepper flakes. Cover with cold water. Bring the mixture to a boil and cook on medium-high heat for 45 minutes, or until the cabbage is tender. Add salt and pepper to taste.

STUFFED CABBAGE LEAVES

MAKES 8 TO 10 SERVINGS

1	POUND GROUND MEAT
$\frac{1}{2}$	CUP CHOPPED ONION
1	(14-OUNCE) CAN BEEF BROTH
1	CUP RICE
1	TEASPOON LEMON PEEL
1	CUP FRUIT (I USE DRIED APRICOTS)
$\frac{1}{4}$	CUP CHOPPED WALNUTS
$\frac{1}{2}$	TEASPOON MINT LEAVES
1	HEAD CABBAGE
1	(10-OUNCE) CAN TOMATO RICE SOUP
$\frac{1}{4}$	TEASPOON GROUND CINNAMON
1	TABLESPOON LEMON JUICE
$\frac{1}{4}$	CUP CHOPPED FRESH PARSLEY

Sauté the meat and onion in a large pot over medium-high heat until well browned. Add the beef broth, rice, and lemon peel. Heat to boiling. Reduce the heat to low. Cover and simmer for about 25 minutes. Add water during cooking if needed. Remove from the heat and stir in the fruit, walnuts, and mint leaves.

Preheat the oven to 350°. Simmer the head of cabbage, covered, on low in a saucepan for 1 to 2 minutes or until the outer leaves are softened. Remove six outer leaves and drain them on paper towels. Cut out any tough stems. Spoon $\frac{1}{4}$ cup meat filling into the center of each leaf. Fold in the sides, and then roll them up from the stem end. Repeat with the remaining leaves. In a bowl stir together the soup, cinnamon, and lemon juice. Pour half the mixture in a baking dish. Place the cabbage rolls, seam side down, on top of the soup mixture. Pour the remaining soup mixture over the rolls and sprinkle with the parsley. Cover with foil and bake for 35 minutes.

SWEET POTATO CASSEROLE

MAKES 10 SERVINGS

CASSEROLE

3	CUPS MASHED SWEET POTATOES
1	CUP SUGAR
2	EGGS, BEATEN
$\frac{1}{2}$	CUP CREAM
2	TEASPOONS SALT
1	TEASPOON VANILLA EXTRACT
1	TEASPOON GROUND CINNAMON
1	TEASPOON GROUND NUTMEG

TOPPING

$\frac{1}{3}$	CUP MELTED BUTTER
1	CUP FIRMLY PACKED DARK BROWN SUGAR
$\frac{1}{2}$	CUP ALL-PURPOSE FLOUR
1	CUP FINELY CHOPPED PECANS OR WALNUTS

Preheat the oven to 350°. For the casserole combine the sweet potatoes, sugar, eggs, cream, salt, vanilla, cinnamon, and nutmeg in a large bowl. Pour into a greased casserole dish. Set aside.

For the topping, mix the butter, brown sugar, flour, and pecans or walnuts together with a fork in a small bowl. Spread over the casserole. Bake in the oven for 30 to 35 minutes.

CORN CASSEROLE

MAKES 8 SERVINGS

1	STICK BUTTER
2	(15-OUNCE) CANS WHITE SHOE PEG CORN, DRAINED
½	PINT WHIPPING CREAM
	SALT AND PEPPER
2	TABLESPOONS ALL-PURPOSE FLOUR

Preheat the oven to 350°. Melt the butter in a baking dish. In a bowl combine the corn, whipping cream, and salt and pepper to taste. Blend in the flour. Pour the mixture into the baking dish and bake for 45 minutes or until lightly browned.

One of Loretta's early performances in the 1960s.

SQUASH CASSEROLE

MAKES 16 SERVINGS

2	POUNDS FRESH SQUASH, CHOPPED
1	LARGE ONION, CHOPPED
2	CUPS SHREDDED AMERICAN CHEESE
2	EGGS, LIGHTLY BEATEN
1	SLEEVE SALTINE CRACKERS
½	STICK BUTTER

Preheat the oven to 350°. In a saucepan cook the squash and onion in water over medium heat until fork tender. Drain the squash and onion. Mix in the cheese and eggs. Pour the mixture into a buttered 13 x 9-inch baking dish. Crush the crackers and sprinkle over the casserole. Melt the butter and pour it over the crackers. Bake for 1 hour or until golden brown.

Loretta in 1960 just after WSM-AM played her first single, "Honky Tonk Girl."

Loretta as a young rising country star in the early 1960s. Photo shot by Oliver "Doolittle" Lynn.

Loretta in the mid-1960s with the personalized guitar she played when writing most of her early hit songs.

Loretta giving a television performance in the late 1970s.

The cover photo from her 1980 album, Loretta.

(Top & Right)
Both of these
were taken in
the late 1970s.

Loretta at her ranch
in Hurricane Mills
in 1982.

(Right & Below)
Loretta Lynn
posing in the
late 1970s.

The cover photo
of Loretta's Just
A Woman *album*
released in 1985.

Loretta at her Hurricane Mills ranch in the late 1970s.

The queen of country on stage in the early 1990s.

Sister Crystal Gayle and Loretta at her Van Leer Rose *album release party in 2004. Photo by Tony Phipps.*

Loretta in 2003 on the front porch of her Hurricane Mills plantation home.

EGGPLANT CASSEROLE

MAKES 6 TO 8 SERVINGS

1	EGGPLANT
$\frac{1}{2}$	LEMON
1	(10-OUNCE) CAN MUSHROOM SOUP
2	CUPS DICED CELERY
1	CUP CHOPPED ONION
20	SODA CRACKERS, CRUSHED
1	(4-OUNCE) CAN SLICED MUSHROOMS
2	EGGS, BEATEN
$\frac{1}{2}$	CUP MILK
3	TABLESPOONS MELTED BUTTER
	DASH OF SALT
1	CUP GRATED CHEDDAR CHEESE

Preheat the oven to 375°. Peel and slice the eggplant. In a saucepan over high heat boil the eggplant with the lemon in salted water just until tender, about 10 minutes. Drain and discard the lemon. In a mixing bowl combine the mushroom soup, celery, onion, cracker crumbs, drained mushrooms, eggs, milk, butter, and salt with the eggplant. Place in a greased casserole dish and sprinkle grated cheese on top. Bake for 1 hour.

ZUCCHINI CASSEROLE

MAKES 10 SERVINGS

3	TABLESPOONS BUTTER
1	MEDIUM ONION, CHOPPED
1	GARLIC CLOVE, MINCED
2	POUNDS COARSELY GRATED ZUCCHINI
$1\frac{1}{2}$	TEASPOONS SALT
2	EGGS
$\frac{1}{2}$	CUP MILK
$\frac{1}{3}$	CUP GRATED CHEDDAR CHEESE
$\frac{1}{2}$	CUP CRUSHED POTATO CHIPS
	PAPRIKA

Preheat the oven to 350°. In a skillet melt the butter over medium-high heat. Add the onion and garlic and cook until tender. Remove the garlic and onion and add the zucchini and salt. Cover and cook until tender and drain. In a large bowl beat together the eggs, milk, and cheese. Stir in the onion, garlic, and zucchini and mix well. Spoon into a $1\frac{1}{2}$-quart baking dish and sprinkle with the crushed potato chips and paprika. Bake for 25 to 30 minutes.

DEVILISH DEVILED EGGS

MAKES 12 SERVINGS

6	LARGE HARD-BOILED EGGS, PEELED
¼	TEASPOON MUSTARD
1	TEASPOON SWEET PICKLE RELISH
1	TEASPOON DILL PICKLE RELISH
1	TABLESPOON MAYONNAISE
	PAPRIKA

Cut the eggs into halves lengthwise. Scoop the yolks into a small mixing bowl. Add the mustard, relishes, and mayo. With a fork, mash and mix all of the ingredients together. With a teaspoon fill the egg whites with the yolk mixture and sprinkle paprika on top.

NOTE: IF YOU DON'T LIKE DILL PICKLE RELISH, YOU CAN USE 2 TEASPOONS OF THE SWEET. PERSONALLY, I LIKE TO USE THEM BOTH.

LORETTA'S HOUSE

If you walked into our house in Butcher Holler, you'd have to go through a bedroom. There was no front room. Mommy had to put beds in it because we didn't have room to have a front room and a bedroom. She would put two beds in each one of the rooms. In the summertime, Mommy would fix it up, kind of close off a little part where the bed was, so that family or somebody, if they come in, wouldn't see the whole house.

Then you'd go through another little room and into the kitchen. They were together, kind of. Mommy had one of those old coal stoves. Daddy would have a fire built in the fireplace, so the place was trying to get warm. Mommy was cooking. That's what I remember. That's the best memory I could remember, you know.

Upstairs we had the curing room. It was a great big room with two long tables. Daddy would salt the meat down and put it up there in the winter. It was so cold, you wouldn't have to worry about it ruining. In the summertime, Mommy would let Junior, my oldest brother, and Herman sleep up there. In the wintertime, it was too cold to sleep up there, so there was nothing up there but the hog meat and maybe some leftover clothes and stuff that Mommy wanted to keep to make quilts out of.

Our well wasn't very far from our home, but our toilet was clear out behind the barn. Let me tell you, you didn't wait 'til you had to go to go. And that's for sure.

I'd get the coal and kindling in a lot of times, make sure that Mommy and Daddy could start the fire at night. Junior, he was a little bit lazy. He'd sit in front of the fire in the wintertime and tell Daddy how big of a watermelon he was going to grow the next year. He was going to have a whole truck bed full of watermelons. He was going to take them to Paintsville. He was going to sell them and get rich.

The next spring, Daddy couldn't get him out with a hoe, let alone get him to work in the garden. I worked in the garden. I hoed corn. I was always behind Daddy. I'd hoe one row, and he'd hoe one row. But he'd always get to his end before I would mine.

Crystal Gayle said to me one day, "I feel bad. I feel like I missed out on a lot by not being born in Butcher Holler." I looked right straight at her and said, "Look at me." I said, "Be happy you didn't live there. Because if you had've, you'd have probably got hungry a few times. Now that's the way it was, whether you want to believe it or not." She didn't miss a dadgum thing.

Loretta (far right on the couch) with her brothers and sisters in the 1970s.

SOUTHERN GREEN BEANS & NEW POTATOES

MAKES 16 SERVINGS

It always tastes best if you can use fresh veggies.

$1\frac{1}{2}$	POUNDS FRESH GREEN BEANS
$\frac{1}{2}$	POUND HOG JOWL OR BACON
6 to 8	SMALL NEW RED POTATOES
2	TABLESPOONS SUGAR
	SALT AND PEPPER

Wash and trim the beans. Break into $1\frac{1}{2}$- to 2-inch pieces. Place in a large pot and cover with water. Add to the beans the jowl or bacon, potatoes, sugar, and salt and pepper to taste. Bring to a full boil for 10 minutes. Reduce the heat and simmer, covered, for about 1 hour and 30 minutes or until the beans are tender, adding water if necessary.

VARIATION: FRESH BEANS MAY BE SUBSTITUTED WITH 1 GALLON OF CANNED BEANS.

HUSH PUPPIES

MAKES 12 SERVINGS

	VEGETABLE OIL FOR FRYING
2	EGGS
1	CUP BUTTERMILK
½	TEASPOON SALT
½	TEASPOON PEPPER
2	CUPS SELF-RISING CORNMEAL
1	WHITE ONION, FINELY CHOPPED

Fill a deep cast-iron skillet with about 3 inches of oil and heat on high heat. In a small bowl mix together the eggs and buttermilk. Add the salt and pepper and mix well. Stir in the cornmeal and onion. Drop the hushpuppy batter into the hot oil by the teaspoon. Fry until the batter turns golden brown. Drain on paper towels.

TURNIP GREENS

MAKES 8 SERVINGS

3	POUNDS TURNIP GREENS
¼	POUND SMOKED BACON
	SALT AND PEPPER

Wash and trim the stems from the turnip greens. Chop the greens into bite-size pieces. Combine the greens and bacon in a saucepan and cover with cold water. Bring to a boil and cook until the greens are tender. Add salt and pepper to taste.

Sisters Peggy Sue, Betty Ruth, Loretta, and Crystal Gayle in the early 1990s.

WHITE BEANS

MAKES 8 SERVINGS

1	POUND DRIED WHITE BEANS
1	LARGE ONION, FINELY CHOPPED
¼	POUND SMOKED BACON
	SALT AND PEPPER

Sort and rinse the beans under cold water. Place the beans in a large pot and cover with cold water. Bring to a boil for 3 minutes. Remove from the heat and let the beans stand for 2 hours to overnight (If soaking overnight, place the beans in the refrigerator). Drain the water from the beans and cover the beans with fresh cold water. Add the onion and bacon to the beans. Simmer for 1½ to 2 hours, until the beans are tender. Add salt and pepper to taste. Cook the beans down until the liquid thickens.

VARIATION: THIS RECIPE WORKS FOR ANY KIND OF DRIED BEAN.

PATCHWORK QUILT RICE

MAKES 4 SERVINGS

3	TABLESPOONS BUTTER
1	CUP SLICED CELERY
1	CUP CHOPPED ONION
$3/4$	CUP CHOPPED CARROTS
$3/4$	CUP CHOPPED GREEN BELL PEPPER
1	CUP CHOPPED TART RED APPLE
1	CUP SLICED MUSHROOMS
1	(6-OUNCE) PACKAGE LONG GRAIN & WILD RICE MIX
1	(10-OUNCE) CAN CHICKEN BROTH
$1/4$	CUP SLIVERED ALMONDS, TOASTED

In a large skillet melt the butter over medium-high heat. Add the celery, onion, carrots, and green pepper. Sauté for 8 minutes or until the carrots are tender. Add the apple and mushrooms and sauté 2 minutes longer. Add the rice from the mix and toss to combine. Stir in the seasoning packet from the mix. In a glass measuring cup combine the chicken broth with enough water to make 2 cups. Stir the broth and water into the rice mixture. Bring to a boil. Reduce the heat and simmer, covered, until the broth is absorbed, about 10 minutes. Stir in the almonds and serve.

MACARONI WITH CHEESE

MAKES 12 SERVINGS

2	POUNDS ELBOW MACARONI
1	STICK BUTTER
3	CUPS SHREDDED CHEDDAR CHEESE
1	CUP SHREDDED SWISS CHEESE
2	CUPS MILK
	SALT AND PEPPER
2	LARGE EGGS, LIGHTLY BEATEN

Preheat the oven to 350°. Cook the macaroni according to the package directions until almost done. Drain and return to the pot. Add the butter and stir until melted. Add the cheddar cheese, Swiss cheese, and milk and mix well. Season with salt and pepper to taste. Stir in the eggs and pour the mixture into a greased casserole dish. Bake for 25 minutes. Serve immediately.

BLANCHE GREEN

After Doo and I had been married about a year, we moved to the state of Washington. I was seven months pregnant. Doo got a job with two brothers, Clyde and Bob Green, who lived near Custer up in the northwest corner of the state. We lived in a little house up there, and I worked in their house. That was my first job.

Clyde and Bob had an aunt, Blanche Smith, who lived with them. Blanche had lived down in Florida, and she cooked for the movie stars. When movie stars went to Florida and stayed two or three months, Blanche cooked for them.

I would go up to the house every day, and Blanche taught me how to cook. Taught me how to cook anything there was to cook. She was what Doo called an "expensive" cook. Anything she wanted, she had to cook with because the two boys that was her nephews was rich. They could have anything they wanted to eat. So Blanche would go into town, and she'd get anything she wanted to cook. And that's where I learned to do my cooking.

Blanche was the one that taught me how to do the beef roast. I'd eat the roast before, but Doo and I didn't never have it. I had never went mushroom hunting before, and her and I went mushroom hunting. And I'd pick strawberries in the summertime then freeze them and can them.

Really, Blanche was the one who taught me everything I know about cooking, things besides beans and potatoes. She taught me how to do chicken and dumplins the way I cook them now, because I do my dumplins a little bit different than Mommy did. Mommy had dip dumplins. I cut mine out. She just dropped little pieces of the dough into her chicken broth. To get really good chicken and dumplins, you have to do them like pie crusts and cut them up into small pieces and drop them into the broth while it's cooking good.

The Greens had beef cattle and milk and butter. That's how I got paid for keeping the house clean and helping her cook. They had these great big tanks that they put the milk in when they milked the cattle. I would clean that out every day. It had to be cleaned and inspected every day that the milk come out of it.

Every now and then, they would give me some meat. And, man, I'll tell you, it was like heaven to get that meat. Doo would spend more money on dadgum shotgun shells for going hunting than it would cost for three beef cows. I told him, "Hey, I don't know why you take so much money for them guns and shells when we could've bought a side of beef." Half the time he wouldn't catch nothing either.

I was pretty well taken care of while I worked for Clyde and Bob. They made sure that my kids eat, and Blanche showed me how to cook. Years later, we went back to visit, and when we left, she said, "Doo, you take my babies away"—there was the kids, and she called me her baby, too—"and I won't live six months." Six months to that day, she died. That broke my heart. The boys, her nephews, sent me a little pocketbook and red hat that she had made herself. I've still got those.

TOMATO PIE

MAKES 6 SERVINGS

2	LARGE TOMATOES, SLICED
1	(9-INCH) UNBAKED PIE SHELL
1	TABLESPOON CHOPPED FRESH BASIL
	SALT AND PEPPER
1	CUP MAYONNAISE
2	CUPS SHREDDED CHEDDAR CHEESE

Preheat the oven to 350°. Place the tomatoes in the pie shell. Sprinkle the basil over the tomatoes. Add salt and pepper to taste. In a small bowl mix together the mayonnaise and cheese. Spread the mixture over the pie. Bake for 30 minutes or until the cheese has melted and turned golden brown.

★ MAIN DISHES ★

CHICKEN-FRIED STEAK WITH GRAVY

CHICKEN & DUMPLINS

BAKED LEMON CHICKEN

CRISPY FRIED CHICKEN

OVEN-FRIED CHICKEN

CREAMY LEMON CHICKEN

CHICKEN & DRESSING

CHICKEN CASSEROLE

CHINESE BEEF CASSEROLE

TUNA CASSEROLE

SALMON CROQUETTES

POOR BOY FILLETS

BEEF ROAST WITH VEGETABLES

BUTCHER HOLLER STEAK

MEATLOAF

OVEN-BARBECUED PORK STEAKS

BARBECUED BEEF OR PORK RIBS

FRIED COUNTRY HAM WITH RED-EYE GRAVY

FRIED PORK CHOPS WITH GRAVY

COUNTRY-FRIED VENISON

STEWED RABBIT

KENTUCKY FROG LEGS

BUTCHER HOLLER POSSUM

FRIED CATFISH

CHICKEN-FRIED STEAK WITH GRAVY

MAKES 4 SERVINGS

CHICKEN FRIED STEAK

1	(16-OUNCE) CAN EVAPORATED MILK
1	EGG
2	POUNDS MINUTE STEAK
1	CUP ALL-PURPOSE FLOUR
2	TABLESPOONS SHORTENING (CRISCO)
	SALT AND PEPPER

GRAVY

$\frac{2}{3}$	CUP STEAK DRIPPINGS
1 to 1$\frac{1}{2}$	TABLESPOONS FLOUR
1	CUP SWEET MILK

In a medium-size bowl mix the evaporated milk and egg together. Dip the steaks one at a time in the egg mixture and then in the flour. Melt the shortening in an iron skillet or frying pan over medium heat. Fry the steaks until each side is golden brown. Add salt and pepper to taste. Remove the steaks from the skillet, reserving $\frac{2}{3}$ cup of the drippings.

For the gravy, mix the reserved drippings with the flour in a small saucepan. Simmer over medium heat. Add the sweet milk and stir until the gravy thickens. Pour over the steak and my Loretta's Mashed Potatoes (page 90). You can't go wrong.

CHICKEN & DUMPLINS

MAKES 6 TO 8 SERVINGS

CHICKEN

1	LARGE FAT HEN, SKINNED
3	GARLIC CLOVES, CRUSHED
	SALT AND PEPPER

DUMPLINS

3	CUPS SELF-RISING FLOUR
1	TEASPOON SALT
1	CUP WATER
1	EGG, BEATEN
6 to 8	CUPS CHICKEN BROTH
$\frac{1}{2}$	CUP CREAM
1	TABLESPOON CORNSTARCH (OPTIONAL)

In a large pot boil the hen with the garlic in water for 2 hours. Add additional water as needed. Drain the hen, reserving the broth. Cut into pieces and discard the bones.

For the dumplins, in a large bowl, sift together the flour and salt. Gradually add the water. Stir in the egg. Knead the dough thoroughly and roll out onto a floured surface. Cut the dough into strips. Bring the chicken broth to a boil and drop the dough into the boiling broth. Cover and simmer for about 10 minutes. Add the cream and chicken pieces and simmer for 5 to 10 minutes longer. Add 1 tablespoon of cornstarch to thicken if needed.

CHICKEN AND DUMPLINS

When Mommy made chicken and dumplins, she would use every part of the chicken. She would boil the chicken feet and peel them. She could take her fingers and pull that first yellow layer of skin from the chickens' feet right off. She would cut off the nails and throw the legs in the dumplins. She said that the chicken legs would have more of a flavor to add to the dumplins. I haven't done that, but Mommy did it all the time.

She'd put the head in the dumplins, too. She would peel off the head, you know. The meat around the head and the brains was what my brother liked. That was his piece of chicken. My piece was the gizzard. There were so many kids, we just had one piece of chicken. That was it.

The first time I tried to make chicken and dumplins for Doo, they wasn't too good. I had went and got cut-up chicken at the store. We didn't have a lot of money at the time, and the chicken didn't cost as much as the other kinds of meat. I thought, "This is great; I don't have to have just beans and stuff. I'll make chicken and dumplins." Well, I had never made them before.

I was putting drop dumplins like my Mommy, and they looked pretty good to me. But they turned out like a whole cooker full of cornbread. Doo liked to have died. He just threw them all out the window.

He threw out everything I cooked for at least three months. I was wondering, "What do you expect out of a fourteen-year-old girl?" Because that summer I turned fourteen. I was thirteen when we got married. Mommy said, "What does he expect out of a kid?" Of course, they wasn't too happy with Doo anyway. Her and Daddy was a little bit mad at him.

Eventually, I learned how to make dumplins the right way, and, years later I made them for Jack White of the White Stripes when he came down to Nashville to work with me on my *Van Lear Rose* album. That time they turned out great. I had green beans and a salad, and I made homemade bread. He really loved that bread. So I made three loaves. I took it out of the oven; it was still warm, and I cut it in great big chunks across. It wasn't like a loaf of bread; it was like three slices at a time. "That's the greatest bread I've ever eaten," he said.

Everybody asks me about my chicken and dumplins now that they know that's what Jack ate when he came down here. Anybody that comes over for dinner, they're likely to get chicken and dumplins. I like to fix it at Christmas, too. It's one of my best dishes.

133

BAKED LEMON CHICKEN

MAKES 4 SERVINGS

1	LARGE HEN
3	LARGE LEMONS
1	STICK BUTTER
	DASH OF SALT
	DASH OF PEPPER
	DASH OF PAPRIKA
1	LARGE WHITE ONION, QUARTERED
2	CELERY STALKS, HALVED
1	GARLIC BULB, PEELED

Preheat the oven to 450°. Wash the hen and pat dry. In a small bowl squeeze the juice from the lemons. Keep the lemons after squeezing out the juice. Melt ½ stick of the butter and add to the lemon juice. Add the salt, pepper, and paprika to the juice. Rub the bird with the remaining ½ stick butter and dust with salt and pepper. Stuff the bird with the onion, celery, reserved lemons, and garlic. Bake in a roasting pan for 20 to 25 minutes. Reduce the heat to 350°. Cover the bird with foil. Continue to bake for 1 hour longer. Baste with the lemon sauce every 10 minutes.

BETTY SUE AND JACK BENNY

When she was little, my oldest daughter, Betty Sue, hated peas. She didn't want no peas. I'd tell her before she went to the table, "Don't say that you don't want no peas, and Doo won't make you eat them." At the table nobody talked. They'd pass their plates around and, as they passed them around, Doo would fill them up. If she'd kept her mouth shut when it was time for peas, she would've not got 'em. But he would fill her plate full of peas every time, and she would cry. And she'd be sitting there for hours not wanting to eat them peas. Sometimes I'd sneak and pour them down the drain for her.

Jack Benny loved the beans. He was kind of like the Webbs, my side of the family. He liked beans and potatoes, and he liked meat, too. But there was nothing he wouldn't eat. There was nothing any of my kids wouldn't eat, except for Betty and her peas. The others would eat anything.

Jack was my oldest boy. He drowned in 1984. I loved that kid so much. He looked just like his daddy, exactly like him. That's what I wanted, a boy that looks like his daddy. Well, that was my second baby. He would listen to what his daddy said one day, and then the next day he'd say it. Him and Doo couldn't get along. They butted heads because they were just alike. Jack would do everything he could to make Doo happy, and he just couldn't do it. There was no way.

Jack loved chicken like my daddy did. He loved the beans. He loved to eat like my daddy. Before the meal was over, Jack would be eating the chicken, and Doo would say, "Eat up, Ted Webb!" Doo was making fun of the way he eat because it was chicken and beans and potatoes instead of maybe something else that was fixed. Jack would cry. And that would ruin the whole meal for me.

Betty Sue, she's a good cook herself. She cooks whatever she wants to cook, and she's good at it. No matter what she cooks, it's good. Jack Benny learned to cook real well, too, but it wasn't no fancy thing.

I'd bought me an iron teakettle once. Jack Benny come in and said, "Mommy, I'd like to have that. That's just what I'd keep on my old wood stove in the wintertime." 'Cause they lived in a little house. So as he started down the stairs, I called his name. He turned around, and I said, "Here," and I give it to him. It tickled him to death that he got that iron teapot.

135

CRISPY FRIED CHICKEN

MAKES 4 SERVINGS

1	($2\frac{1}{2}$- TO 3-POUND) CHICKEN, CUT UP

SEASONED FLOUR

$1\frac{1}{2}$	CUPS FLOUR
1	TABLESPOON GARLIC SALT
$1\frac{1}{2}$	TEASPOONS PEPPER
$1\frac{1}{2}$	TEASPOONS PAPRIKA
$\frac{1}{4}$	TEASPOON POULTRY SEASONING

CRISPY BATTER

$\frac{2}{3}$	CUP FLOUR
$\frac{1}{2}$	TEASPOON SALT
$\frac{1}{8}$	TEASPOON PEPPER
1	EGG YOLK, BEATEN
$\frac{3}{4}$	CUP WATER
	SHORTENING (CRISCO) FOR FRYING

Rinse the chicken and pat dry.

For the seasoned flour, combine the flour, garlic salt, pepper, paprika, and poultry seasoning in a small bowl. Set the mixture aside.

For the crispy batter, combine the flour, salt, pepper, egg yolk, and water in a medium bowl. Fill a skillet about halfway up with shortening and heat over medium-high heat to 365°. Dip the chicken in the seasoned flour, then into the crispy batter, and again into the seasoned flour. Fry the chicken in the shortening for 15 to 18 minutes or until crisp and well browned. Drain on paper towels.

CRISCO DAYS

In the late 1970s, my manager at the time, David Skepner, was approached by Procter & Gamble to ask me to be the spokeswoman for Crisco shortening. I guess David had shown them an old photo of me taken when I won the blue ribbon at the county fair in Washington state. In the picture, bigger than day, sat an old can of Crisco. I used it then and still use it now. The Crisco spokeswoman years were a great time for me.

Loretta in the kitchen in Washington in the mid 1950s.

The commercials started right before the release of the movie *Coal Miner's Daughter*, and we made the commercials for many years. I loved the fact that my own kids got to be in most of the commercials. What you may not know is that most of the commercials were filmed in my own kitchen at my home in Hurricane Mills. Doolittle loved making the Crisco commercials more than all of us put together. He truly was the big ham of the family.

I remember one funny story. While we were filming one of the commercials, the set design crew had built a fake wall with a window. Doolittle was supposed to act like he was going to lean through this fake window to reach and grab one of my fresh baked cherry pies. Now I guess they must not have nailed that wall down good enough because the minute Doo leaned out that window, grabbed the pie, smiled at the camera and said "Mmmm," he lost his balance, fell out the window with pie in hand, and the whole wall fell on top of him.

Doo was fine, embarrassed more than anything. Now I couldn't help but kind of get a kick out of Doo falling through that window. Talkin' about pie in your face.

Every now and then, me and the twins love going back and watching those old commercials, seeing me and Doo together . . . what happy, happy memories.

OVEN-FRIED CHICKEN

MAKES 6 SERVINGS

1	MEDIUM FRYER, CUT UP
2	TEASPOONS SALT
¼	CUP ITALIAN SALAD DRESSING
1½	CUPS CRUSHED CORN FLAKES

Preheat the oven to 375°. Rinse the chicken and pat dry. Season with the salt. Dip the chicken in the salad dressing and then roll it in the corn flakes. Arrange the chicken skin side up in a 13 x 9-inch baking dish lined with foil. Bake for 1 hour.

*Loretta signing autographs after
a show in the 1970s.*

CREAMY LEMON CHICKEN

MAKES 4 SERVINGS

1	STICK BUTTER
	SALT AND PEPPER
4	(7-OUNCE) BONELESS, SKINLESS CHICKEN BREASTS
1	CUP MAYONNAISE
1	CUP SOUR CREAM
¼	CUP LEMON JUICE
¼	CUP SHREDDED CHEDDAR CHEESE

Preheat the oven to 375°. Melt the butter in a medium skillet over medium-high heat. Rub the salt and pepper over the chicken breasts and brown on both sides. Place in an 8 x 2-inch baking dish. In a bowl combine the mayonnaise, sour cream, and lemon juice and pour over the chicken. Sprinkle the cheddar cheese on top and bake for 30 minutes.

CHICKEN & DRESSING

MAKES 10 SERVINGS

HEN

1	LARGE (5- TO 7-POUND) HEN
2	CELERY STALKS, COARSELY CHOPPED
$\frac{1}{4}$	CUP CHOPPED ONION
	SALT AND PEPPER

DRESSING

$1\frac{1}{2}$	CUPS BUTTERMILK
2 plus 2	EGGS, BEATEN
3	CUPS SELF-RISING CORNMEAL
2	TABLESPOONS VEGETABLE OIL
1	STICK BUTTER
4	STALKS CELERY, CHOPPED
$\frac{3}{4}$	CUP CHOPPED ONION
4	SLICES DRY BREAD
1	SLEEVE SALTINE CRACKERS, FINELY CRUSHED
2	TABLESPOONS SALT
2	TABLESPOONS BLACK PEPPER
1	TABLESPOON SAGE
2 to 3	CUPS RESERVED CHICKEN BROTH

In a large pot combine the hen, celery, and onion with enough cold water to cover. Add salt and pepper to taste. Boil for 1½ to 2 hours or until the hen is done and the meat is pulling away from the bone. Drain and set the hen aside. Reserve the broth for the dressing.

For the dressing, preheat the oven to 450°. In a bowl mix the buttermilk and 2 of the eggs together. Add the cornmeal and stir until well combined. Pour the oil into a cast-iron skillet and heat in the oven. When the oil is very hot, remove the skillet and pour in the cornbread batter. Bake for 25 minutes or until golden brown. Remove the cornbread from the oven and set aside.

Reduce the temperature to 400°. Melt the butter in another skillet. Sauté the celery and onion until the celery is soft and the onion is translucent. Crumble the cornbread and dry bread into a large bowl. Add the celery, onion, crackers, salt, pepper, and sage. Mix well and then add enough of the reserved broth to form a very loose and wet mixture. In a separate bowl mix the remaining 2 eggs with the dressing. Pour the mixture into a greased 13 x 9-inch baking dish. Bake until golden brown. Serve warm with the hen. The hen may be served carved, but it's just as good torn up into pieces and scattered over the top of the dressing.

CLEANIN' CHICKENS

In the sixties, right after Doo and I bought Hurricane Mills, Doo's parents—Red and Angie—came to live down there for a couple of years. We had a chicken house out behind the main house, and in the springtime we killed the chickens.

Jack Benny would cut the heads off, then he would pass the chickens on to Pat, his wife, and she would dip them in hot water. I would pluck them and gut them and then pass them on down to Doo's mom. She would cut them up. They were fryers. We had an assembly line going. We'd put up a hundred a day like that.

I had my overalls—I call them "overhauls"—on, and they were rolled up to my knees. There was blood all over my face, and my hair was put back on top of my head. This woman and her husband came in while we were killing these chickens, and they said, "We come to see Loretta Lynn."

"She's not here," Doo told them. "She's on the road."

"Well, we wanted to see her so bad," they said. "We'd know her anywhere. There's no way that we could ever see her and not recognize her." Meanwhile, I'm standing there with blood all over me, running down my shirt, down my legs. I looked a mess. I just kept my head down and kept right on gutting them chickens.

This went on for a while. Finally, Doolittle got tired of it. He grabbed one of them chickens, picked up an axe, and cut the chicken's head off. The woman fainted.

That was the end of that story.

142

CHICKEN CASSEROLE

MAKES 8 SERVINGS

6	LARGE CHICKEN BREASTS, BOILED AND CUT UP
2	CUPS COOKED RICE
1	(10-OUNCE) CAN CREAM OF CHICKEN SOUP
1	(10-OUNCE) CAN CREAM OF MUSHROOM SOUP
8	OUNCES SOUR CREAM
$\frac{1}{4}$	CUP WHITE COOKING WINE
1	EGG, BEATEN
1	CUP SHREDDED CHEDDAR CHEESE
3	CUPS CRACKER CRUMBS (RITZ WORKS THE BEST)
1	STICK BUTTER, CUT INTO SMALL PIECES
	PAPRIKA

Preheat the oven to 350°. In a large bowl combine the chicken, rice, chicken soup, mushroom soup, sour cream, wine, and egg. Pour the mixture into a buttered 13 x 9-inch casserole dish. Sprinkle the cheese over the casserole and top with the cracker crumbs. Arrange the butter on top. Sprinkle with paprika. Bake for 40 minutes.

CHINESE BEEF CASSEROLE

MAKES 8 SERVINGS

1	POUND GROUND BEEF
1	(10-OUNCE) PACKAGE FROZEN PEAS, THAWED
2	CUPS FINELY SLICED CELERY
1	(10-OUNCE) CAN BEAN SPROUTS, DRAINED
1	(10-OUNCE) CAN MUSHROOM SOUP
2	TABLESPOONS CREAM OR MILK
1	TEASPOON SALT
½	TEASPOON PEPPER
1	SMALL ONION, CHOPPED
1	CUP CRUSHED POTATO CHIPS

Preheat the oven to 350°. Brown the beef in a skillet until crumbly. Turn into a 2½-quart greased casserole dish. Add the peas, celery, bean sprouts, mushroom soup, cream or milk, salt, pepper, and onion. Mix well. Sprinkle the potato chips on top and bake for 1 hour.

TUNA CASSEROLE

MAKES 8 SERVINGS

8	OUNCES EGG NOODLES
1	(10-OUNCE) CAN CREAM OF MUSHROOM SOUP
1	(8-OUNCE) CONTAINER SOUR CREAM
2	(6-OUNCE) CANS TUNA
$\frac{1}{2}$	CUP SLICED GREEN OLIVES
$\frac{1}{2}$	TEASPOON SALT
2	CUPS SHREDDED CHEDDAR CHEESE
	PAPRIKA

Preheat the oven to 350°. Cook the noodles according to the package directions until almost done. They should still be a little bit firm. While the noodles are cooking, mix together the soup, sour cream, tuna, olives, and salt in a large bowl. After the noodles are done, drain and add to the tuna mixture. Pour the mixture into a buttered 13 x 9-inch casserole dish. Top with the cheddar cheese and sprinkle with the paprika. Cover the casserole with foil and bake for 30 minutes. Remove the foil and bake until the cheese starts to brown.

SALMON CROQUETTES

MAKES 8 SERVINGS

1	(14¾-OUNCE) CAN PINK SALMON, DRAINED
1½	CUPS MASHED POTATOES
1	SMALL ONION, GRATED
1	EGG, LIGHTLY BEATEN
½	TEASPOON BLACK PEPPER
¼	CUP DRY BREADCRUMBS
3	TABLESPOONS VEGETABLE OIL

In a large bowl combine the salmon, mashed potatoes, onion, egg, and pepper and mix well. Shape into eight patties, each about ¾-inch thick. Spread the breadcrumbs on wax paper. Gently press the patties in the crumbs, coating both sides. Heat the oil in a large skillet over medium heat. Add the patties and cook for 4 minutes on each side or until heated through, golden, and crisp.

POOR BOY FILLETS

MAKES 8 SERVINGS

1	POUND GROUND BEEF
1	(4-OUNCE) CAN MUSHROOM STEMS AND PIECES
$\frac{1}{4}$	CUP GRATED PARMESAN CHEESE
$\frac{1}{2}$	TEASPOON LEMON-PEPPER SEASONING
3	TABLESPOONS FINELY CHOPPED PIMIENTO-STUFFED OLIVES
2	TABLESPOONS CHOPPED GREEN BELL PEPPER
2	TABLESPOONS CHOPPED ONION
$\frac{1}{2}$	TEASPOON SALT
6	SLICES BACON

Pat the ground beef into a 12 x 7-inch rectangular pan lined with wax paper. In a bowl mix the mushrooms, cheese, lemon-pepper, olives, green pepper, onion, and salt together. Spread evenly over the beef. Roll as for a jelly roll, sealing the edges and ends. Place seam side down onto a baking sheet. Smooth and shape the beef roll using your hands. Cover and refrigerate for 2 to 3 hours. Cook the bacon in a skillet over medium heat until limp but not brown; drain. Cut the beef roll into 1½-inch-thick slices. Wrap a slice of bacon around the edge of each beef slice. Secure with a wooden toothpick. Grill the beef slices over hot coals for 8 minutes on each side or until the degree of doneness desired.

BEEF ROAST

About six weeks after I got married, Doo's mother made the first beef roast I ever ate. It was the first time I'd ever seen beef. In those doggone hills where I lived you couldn't raise no cows. There was one little flat place, and that's where Mommy always kept her garden. So there was no beef. Daddy had one milk cow. That's where we got the milk and butter. Mommy would make me churn every day, just about. I loved to churn.

Well, Doo's mother and father, they could get beef, and she had more to cook with than my mother. Doo's mother would put the beef in a skillet, and she'd brown it on both sides. She'd salt and pepper it on both sides. She'd stick in a roaster and put it in the oven. Just before it got done, she'd put onions, potatoes, and carrots in and stick it back in the oven. By the time they were soft, the meat was done. Out they would come, and we'd eat. It was a very easy recipe, but that was the best meat I ever had. I thought, "Gee, this is good."

I told Mommy it was out of this world. I said, "Mommy, I've eat cow meat." She said, "Oh, what do you mean?" I said, "I've eat cow meat." She said: "No, you haven't. They don't kill cows. Cows are for milking, Loretta." And I said, "Mommy, I swear they had a beef roast. They told me this roast was from a cow." She couldn't believe it. I don't know whether she ever believed me or not. But that was the first time I'd ever eat beef, was after I got married.

Doo, second from the right beside his mother, Angie, and his brothers and sisters in the 1930s.

BEEF ROAST WITH VEGETABLES

MAKES 6 TO 8 SERVINGS

1	(3- TO 4-POUND) ROUND OR RUMP ROAST
	SALT AND PEPPER
1	POUND POTATOES, CUT LENGTHWISE INTO QUARTERS
1	POUND CARROTS, CUT INTO LARGE PIECES
1	LARGE ONION, QUARTERED
1	TABLESPOON ALL-PURPOSE FLOUR
½	CUP COLD WATER

Preheat the oven to 350°. Rinse the roast and pat dry. Rub the roast generously with salt and pepper and let stand. Heat a large skillet over high heat. When hot, sear the roast on all sides. Place the roast in a large baking pan and cover with foil. Bake for 3½ to 4 hours. During the last hour of cooking, add the potatoes, carrots, and onion and enough water to cover. Add salt and pepper to taste. When the vegetables are tender, remove the roast from the oven and pour the liquid into a saucepan. In a small bowl mix the flour with the cold water and add to the liquid from the roast. Boil for 5 minutes and then return the liquid mixture to the roast and veggies.

BUTCHER HOLLER STEAK

MAKES 4 TO 6 SERVINGS

¼	CUP ALL-PURPOSE FLOUR
1	TABLESPOON BLACK PEPPER
¼	TABLESPOON GARLIC POWDER
1	STICK UNSALTED BUTTER
½	CUP VEGETABLE OIL
1 to 1½	POUNDS CHOPPED STEAK
1	LARGE WHITE ONION, CHOPPED
1	TABLESPOON KETCHUP
1	TABLESPOON BROWN SUGAR
1	TABLESPOON DRY MUSTARD
¼	CUP WATER

In a bowl combine the flour, pepper, and garlic powder. Melt the butter in a large skillet over high heat. Add the oil and continue to heat until hot, approximately 325°. Dredge the steaks through the flour mixture and place them in the skillet. Add the onion and brown the steaks on both sides. Add the ketchup, brown sugar, mustard, and water. Reduce the heat to low and simmer, covered, for about 20 minutes. Remove the lid and simmer for 15 minutes longer.

MEATLOAF

MAKES 8 SERVINGS

2	POUNDS GROUND BEEF
1	SMALL ONION, FINELY CHOPPED
1	EGG, BEATEN
1	SLEEVE SALTINE CRACKERS, FINELY CRUSHED
1	TEASPOON GARLIC POWDER
1	TEASPOON ITALIAN SEASONING
1	CUP KETCHUP
½	CUP FIRMLY PACKED BROWN SUGAR

Preheat the oven to 350°. In a large bowl mix together the ground beef, onion, egg, crackers, garlic powder, and Italian seasoning. Shape the mixture into a loaf and place in a loaf pan. Bake for 1 hour. In a small bowl combine the ketchup and brown sugar. Pour over the meatloaf and bake for an additional 30 minutes.

OVEN-BARBECUED PORK STEAKS

MAKES 6 SERVINGS

$\frac{1}{4}$	CUP BROWN SUGAR
$\frac{1}{4}$	CUP KETCHUP
1	TABLESPOON ONION POWDER
$\frac{1}{4}$	TEASPOON SALT
$\frac{1}{4}$	TEASPOON BLACK PEPPER
6	PORK LOIN STEAK CHOPS
$\frac{1}{4}$	CUP WATER
1	MEDIUM WHITE ONION, SLICED

Preheat the oven to 350°. In a bowl combine the sugar, ketchup, onion powder, salt, and pepper. Pour over the chops and place them in a 9 x 13-inch baking dish. Add the water and the sliced onion. Cover tightly with foil and bake for 1½ hours. Remove the foil, turn the chops, and bake for about 20 minutes longer.

CHRISTMAS AS A KID

We usually had one hog, and Daddy would kill it before Christmas. Then we'd have backbones and ribs, and for breakfast we'd have hog meat. That was a real treat because otherwise it was just gravy and biscuits and whatever Mommy had.

When Christmas come around, we got peanuts and an apple and some hard candy, that is, if we were lucky. One time, we didn't get nothing. I was five years old. I remember getting up out of bed, and I was just crying. Mommy told me, "Loretty, you hush that crying. Santy Claus can't get here." I asked her why. I was just crying, you know. She said, "It's snowing outside, and the snow's too deep. He can't get here." About that time, the door come open, and this guy come in. He had a bandana around his face, and this little old cap with a bill on it. He come over to the bed where I was and poured out some hard candy. I said, "See, Mommy? I told you Santa Claus was going to come!" Really, it was my cousin Lee Dollarhide. He'd robbed the candy store. That was one of the great Christmases I remember.

Christmas dinner wasn't any different than any other day. Christmas Eve's what we liked. That's when we got to see what was going to happen. One Christmas Eve after Daddy started working in the mine, I remember Jay Lee, my brother, he got a tricycle. I got a little doll. One of my brothers got a little wagon. Man, we were in high heaven at that time.

Loretta's brother Jay Lee, Doo, and Loretta in Washington in the 1950s.

BARBECUED BEEF OR PORK RIBS

MAKES 4 SERVINGS

BARBECUE SAUCE

$\frac{1}{2}$	CUP VINEGAR
2	TABLESPOONS FIRMLY PACKED BROWN SUGAR
$\frac{1}{2}$	CUP KETCHUP
1	TABLESPOON DRY MUSTARD
$\frac{1}{4}$	CUP LEMON JUICE
2	TABLESPOONS WORCESTERSHIRE SAUCE
1	SMALL ONION, CHOPPED
1	TABLESPOON MINCED GARLIC
	DASH OF SALT
2	POUNDS PORK OR BEEF RIBS

For the sauce, in a bowl mix the vinegar, brown sugar, ketchup, dry mustard, lemon juice, Worcestershire sauce, onion, garlic, and salt until well blended.

Preheat the oven to 450°. Place the ribs in a well-greased baking dish. Pour the barbecue sauce over the ribs. Cover with foil. Bake for 15 to 20 minutes. Reduce the temperature to 350° and bake for 1 hour and 30 minutes longer.

FRIED COUNTRY HAM WITH RED-EYE GRAVY

MAKES 6 SERVINGS

12	OUNCES COUNTRY HAM SLICES
2	CUPS STRONG BLACK COFFEE (INSTANT WORKS GOOD, TOO)
	SALT

Fry the ham in a cast-iron skillet over medium-low heat. Fry it slowly so all the fat melts off into the pan. As the ham starts to fry, turn up the heat so it starts to brown. As soon as the ham has finished cooking, remove it from the skillet and pour in the coffee. Watch out for the steam! Simmer the coffee for about 1 minute. Salt to taste. Serve with hot biscuits.

FRIED PORK CHOPS WITH GRAVY

MAKES 4 SERVINGS

$\frac{1}{2}$	CUP VEGETABLE OIL
1	POUND FRESH PORK CHOPS
	SALT AND PEPPER
1	CUP PLUS 1 TABLESPOON ALL-PURPOSE FLOUR
2	CUPS MILK

In a cast-iron skillet preheat the oil to 350°. Rinse the pork chops and pat dry. Rub with salt and pepper. Dredge the pork chops in 1 cup of the flour. Place the pork chops in the skillet and fry until golden brown on each side. Remove the chops from the skillet and drain the excess oil. Add the remaining 1 tablespoon flour to the skillet. Stir in the milk. Add salt and pepper to taste. Cook for 3 minutes over medium-high heat. Serve the gravy over the pork chops.

COUNTRY-FRIED VENISON

MAKES 4 TO 6 SERVINGS

1 to 2	POUNDS DEER STEAKS
$\frac{1}{2}$	PLUS $\frac{1}{2}$ CUP ALL-PURPOSE FLOUR
2	TEASPOONS SALT
1	TEASPOON PEPPER
$\frac{1}{4}$	CUP SHORTENING
1	CUP HOT WATER

Cut the deer steaks thin. In a bowl combine $\frac{1}{2}$ cup of the flour with the salt and pepper. Dredge the meat in the flour mixture. Heat the shortening in a cast-iron skillet over high heat until sizzling. Brown the steaks on both sides, 5 to 6 minutes on each side. Remove the steaks and drain all but about 2 tablespoons of oil from the pan. Return the pan to the heat and add the remaining flour. Brown the remaining flour for about 1 minute and then add the hot water. Stir until smooth. Add the steaks, reduce the heat to medium low, and simmer for about 20 minutes.

STEWED RABBIT

MAKES 8 SERVINGS

6 to 8	QUARTS WATER
4 to 5	RABBITS (ABOUT 1 POUND EACH)
5	STALKS CELERY, CHOPPED
1	LARGE ONION, QUARTERED
1	(16-OUNCE) CAN CHOPPED TOMATOES
10 to 12	MEDIUM POTATOES, CUBED
2	TABLESPOONS FLOUR
	SALT AND PEPPER

In a large pot over high heat bring the water to a boil. Add the rabbits, celery, and onion. Simmer on low heat for 2½ hours. Remove the rabbits from the pot and set aside. Add the tomatoes and potatoes to the pot. Remove the rabbit meat from its bone and dust with flour. Add the rabbit meat back to the pot and salt and pepper to taste. Simmer for about 1 hour.

PATSY CLINE AND RABBIT

Patsy Cline loved rabbit. She liked the wild rabbit, not the kind you can go to a store and get. You can fry rabbit just like chicken. I would fix it for her just like that. I would skin the rabbit. Sometimes little hairs got on the meat, so I would make sure it was real clean before I cut it up. Then I'd bread it, put it in a hot skillet of grease and fry it. We'd probably eat it together once a week.

The Thursday before she was killed, she came over after dinner to put curtains up in my house. The kids and Doo had gotten through eating, but I hadn't got the dishes off the table. She went by the table, she seen the rabbit there, and she grabbed a piece of rabbit and started eating on that thing. She eat that piece and had another one 'fore she left.

When I come to Nashville, we were eating wild meat, beans, and potatoes. Doo would go out and hunt for rabbit and possum. I guess he would tell Patsy when he was going hunting, because every time I'd have it, she ended up at my house.

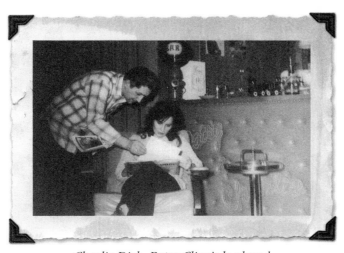

Charlie Dick, Patsy Cline's husband,
and Loretta in 1962.

159

CHRISTMAS WITH THE LYNNS

One Christmas while we was out in Washington, I got flatware. The kids would take out my spoons and stuff and dig in the dirt with them, and they'd lose them. So I got a set of spoons and knives and forks. Jack got holsters and a little gun. So did my second boy, Ernest Ray. And maybe there'd be a couple different kinds of candy.

The first Christmas after I started making some money, that was a mess. I didn't mind the Christmas, I just hated the mess, cleaning up the place. The kids got anything they wanted. There wasn't nothing that they could eat that they didn't get. That was a bad thing, I think. I think it's nice to want just a little bit. When you get to where you don't want anymore, you know it's bad. When your kids come in and say, "I want a car for Christmas," you know it's bad.

The whole family still comes in every Thanksgiving and every Christmas. And I still cook for them. Everybody comes into the kitchen, but I shoo them into the front room. Sometimes, we'll do potluck. One'll bring sweet potatoes with nuts in them and fixed up real pretty. Cissie usually fixes sweet potatoes because she knows I love them. Betty, she can cook anything she wants to. You've got to know what she's going to bring. Whatever Ernest and his wife bring, you can bet it'll be something good because she's a good little cook.

I cook the turkey and dressing. I put oysters in my dressing. The oysters make it more moist, but you can't taste them like you can by themselves. I cook the turkey and the dressing, green beans, and corn. Whatever I have in the house, they get.

KENTUCKY FROG LEGS

MAKES 4 SERVINGS

	VEGETABLE OIL
8	FROG LEGS
¼	CUP ALL-PURPOSE FLOUR
1	CUP CRACKER CRUMBS
1	EGG, BEATEN
	SALT AND PEPPER

In a large skillet heat 3 to 4 inches of vegetable oil over high heat. Wash the frog legs in cold water. Skin the legs and rinse in cold water again. Dry the legs completely. In a bowl combine the flour and cracker crumbs. Dip the frog legs in the egg and then dredge in the flour mixture. Fry the frog legs in the hot oil for 3 to 4 minutes. Remove from the oil, place on paper towels, and sprinkle with salt and pepper to taste.

POSSUM

At night, Mommy would go out and set traps. She'd take one of the kids with her. Sometimes she took me, but most of the time she'd take the oldest boy—Junior, my eldest brother. They would go out with a light; one of them would track them dadgum animals down, and she'd set that trap. She usually got a possum or a rabbit or a coon every time she went out, so we'd have meat probably once a week.

We had nothing to eat, and we had to get along the best we could. Daddy would grow potatoes and put them in a hole in the ground so we could keep them. He would cover it with straw. I'm the one that went out and got the potatoes out of the hole for Mommy to cook or fry in the wintertime. I knew exactly how to put the dirt back over them, and then put the straw back over that, and a great big piece of tin. That's the way Daddy kept his turnips, his onions, and his potatoes. By springtime, we'd be completely out. We'd just be eating beans, beans without potatoes. He would try to raise enough to put in there for most of the winter.

I know people will holler, but possum was my Daddy's favorite dish. If they lived where I lived, they would think it was a great dish, too.

Possum is a different tasting meat than anything I've ever tasted. To me, it was kind of oily, greasy, but Daddy loved it. Mommy would have to cook it like three hours first, because it's tough. Then she'd take it out and put it in a pan. She'd peel the sweet potatoes, and she'd put 'em around the possum. And when the sweet potatoes was done, so was the possum. That's what Daddy loved.

BUTCHER HOLLER POSSUM

MAKES 6 SERVINGS

1	GOOD-SIZE POSSUM
	SALT AND PEPPER
$\frac{1}{2}$	CUP BREADCRUMBS
$\frac{1}{2}$	CUP APPLESAUCE
$\frac{1}{2}$	CUP CHOPPED CHESTNUTS
$\frac{1}{2}$	STICK BUTTER, THINLY SLICED
4	SWEET POTATOES, CUBED
	OR CUT INTO $\frac{1}{2}$-INCH-THICK PIECES
1	CUP WATER
$\frac{1}{2}$	CUP LEMON JUICE

Preheat the oven to 350°. Skin and clean the possum by removing all the innards. Scrape the inside clean and scald in boiling water. Season the inside with salt and pepper to taste. Mix the breadcrumbs, applesauce, and chestnuts in a bowl. Stuff the breadcrumb mixture and butter slices inside the possum. Place in a Dutch oven. Add the sweet potatoes, water, and lemon juice. Bake in the oven until tender, basting often.

DOO AND HIS FOOD

When we first got married, Doo didn't like my cooking at all. He would throw out everything I would cook, telling me I couldn't cook. He'd throw it off the porch, and our dog, Drive, would eat it. I never cooked anything so bad Drive wouldn't eat it. That dog got so fat he couldn't get up off the ground.

I thought I was a pretty good cook. I could fix beans, potatoes, and cornbread. Now, biscuits I was not too good on. I am now, but at that time I was not baking too great of a biscuit. Doo didn't say too much about them, but he didn't eat them either. I think he eat about half of one. I just had to learn as I went along, so it would be one thing at a time. I'd mess up on them the first time, and . . . sometimes, the second time, too. But I tried.

At that time, though, we didn't have no big selection. When I was a little girl, it had been beans and taters or taters and beans. Daddy had sweet potatoes sometimes, and Mommy would fry sweet potatoes, or she would bake them. We'd eat whatever there was to eat. That's why I didn't know how to cook much when I got married. I had never fixed anything but beans and taters. But that didn't matter to Doo anyway. He had another girlfriend; that was the problem.

Doo's mom, she come down one time early before he got home. She cooked beans and fried potatoes. She did it just exactly like I was doing it, only she was doing it her way. Doo threw that out, too. So we knew then there was more to it than just cooking.

He had a girlfriend in Paintsville, Kentucky, so this is why he kept throwing out the food. He thought he could just up and leave me, and me pregnant. That's what he did—he run me off at ten o'clock one night. But I wasn't alone too long 'til he was coming back. Still, it's hard to learn how to cook when you've got an unfaithful husband who's got another girl.

Doo got to be a good cook himself, eventually. He always liked to take a copy of *The Joy of Cooking* with him when we went somewhere. He folded down the pages of the recipes he wanted to try. But he could come up with some pretty terrible concoctions, too.

164

I'll never forget one time we was in Mexico. (We had a home down there.) Doolittle caught this fish, and he said he was going to cook up a slumgullion. That's what he called it, and, boy, that's how it tasted, too. I don't know what the heck he done to it. I have no idea what he put in it. That was the first time I ever saw Doo make something that he couldn't eat. The housekeeper, she was going to eat it or die to make Doolittle think that she liked it. The first thing you know, she was in the bathroom vomiting like everything. I said, "Listen to her, Doo. And then you're trying to make us eat this stuff." We ended up throwing it out into the yard. There were wild iguanas everywhere out there, but that stuff sat in a pan in the yard for four days. Not even an iguana would come over to eat it.

Loretta's husband Oliver "Doolittle" Lynn.

165

FRIED CATFISH

MAKES 8 SERVINGS

$1\frac{1}{2}$	CUPS YELLOW CORNMEAL
$\frac{1}{4}$	CUP ALL-PURPOSE FLOUR
3	TEASPOONS SALT
3	TEASPOONS PEPPER
8	CATFISH FILLETS
	VEGETABLE OIL FOR FRYING

In a small bowl mix the cornmeal, flour, salt, and pepper together. Rinse the fish and pat dry. Dredge the fish in the dry mixture and shake off the excess. Fill a large cast-iron skillet with oil and heat to about 350°. Fry the fish in the oil for about 4 minutes on each side or until golden brown. Drain on paper towels. Serve hot.

★ DESSERTS ★

OLD-FASHIONED OATMEAL COOKIES

MOMMY'S SUNDAY COOKIES

BUTTERNUT CHEWIES

LORETTA'S BEST PEANUT BUTTER FUDGE

BUTTERMILK PIE

FUDGE PIE

OLD-FASHIONED MOLASSES PIE

LORETTA'S FAVORITE CHOCOLATE PIE

SOUTHERN SOFT CUSTARD

OLD-FASHIONED BREAD PUDDING

BANANA PUDDING

CHOCOLATE & MARSHMALLOW CAKE

CHOCOLATE & MARSHMALLOW CAKE ICING

GOOEY CAKE

HOMEMADE PEACH CAKE

LEMON WHIPPERSNAPPERS

STRAWBERRY & RHUBARB PIE

APPLE TURNOVERS

FROSTED PECANS

FUDGE CANDY

FRUIT ICE

OLD-FASHIONED OATMEAL COOKIES

MAKES 2 DOZEN

2	CUPS SUGAR
$\frac{1}{2}$	CUP COCOA
$\frac{1}{2}$	CUP SWEET MILK
1	STICK BUTTER (OR MARGARINE)
3	CUPS UNCOOKED OATS
1	TEASPOON VANILLA EXTRACT

Preheat the oven to 350°. In a medium saucepan combine the sugar, cocoa, and sweet milk. Boil for 1 minute. Remove from the heat and add the butter, oats, and vanilla. Stir until almost cool. Cover a cookie sheet with wax paper. Drop tablespoonfuls of batter onto the cookie sheet. Bake for 10 to 12 minutes or until done to taste.

VARIATION: YOU CAN ALSO ADD PEANUT BUTTER WHEN YOU ADD THE BUTTER, OATS, AND VANILLA. I LOVE PEANUT BUTTER.

MOMMY'S SUNDAY COOKIES

MAKES 3 TO 4 DOZEN

2	CUPS SIFTED ALL-PURPOSE FLOUR
2	TEASPOONS BAKING POWDER
$\frac{1}{2}$	TEASPOON SALT
2	EGGS
$\frac{3}{4}$	CUP BUTTER, SOFTENED
2	TEASPOONS VANILLA EXTRACT
1	CUP SUGAR PLUS SOME FOR DIPPING

Preheat the oven to 350°. In a medium mixing bowl combine the flour, baking powder, and salt. In a small mixing bowl beat the eggs on low. Beat in the butter and vanilla. Beat in 1 cup of the sugar and the dry mix until thick. Drop the batter by teaspoonfuls onto an ungreased cookie sheet. Dip the bottom of a drinking glass into water and then into a small bowl of sugar. Press each cookie flat. Bake for 8 to 10 minutes.

BUTTERNUT CHEWIES

MAKES 2 DOZEN

2	EGGS
2	CUPS FIRMLY PACKED LIGHT BROWN SUGAR
1	TEASPOON VANILLA EXTRACT
$\frac{1}{2}$	CUP BUTTER-FLAVORED CRISCO, MELTED
$1\frac{1}{2}$	CUPS UNSIFTED ALL-PURPOSE FLOUR
2	TEASPOONS BAKING POWDER
$\frac{1}{2}$	TEASPOON SALT
1	CUP CHOPPED NUTS

Preheat the oven to 350°. Grease a 13 x 9 x 2-inch pan. In a large bowl with an electric mixer beat the eggs until light and foamy. Beat in the brown sugar, vanilla, and Crisco until creamy. In a medium bowl combine the flour, baking powder, and salt. Add the flour mixture to the egg mixture and beat at low speed until blended. Mix in the nuts. The batter will be stiff. Spread the batter evenly in a 13 x 9-inch baking pan. Bake for 25 to 30 minutes or until the top is light brown. Cool for 10 to 15 minutes. Cut into squares.

LORETTA'S BEST PEANUT BUTTER FUDGE

MAKES 24 SQUARES

3	CUPS SUGAR
1	TEASPOON COCOA
¾	CUP WATER
1	STICK BUTTER
1	TEASPOON VANILLA EXTRACT
1	CUP SMOOTH PEANUT BUTTER

In a large bowl mix the sugar and cocoa well. In a saucepan bring the water to a boil over high heat. Reduce the heat to medium and add the cocoa mixture. Cook to soft-ball stage or about 10 minutes. Reduce the heat to low and add the butter and vanilla. Stir until the butter melts. Remove the pan from the heat and quickly add the peanut butter. Stir just until blended. Pour immediately into a greased 9 x 9 x 2-inch baking pan. Score 1-inch squares while warm. Let cool about 20 minutes and cut when firm.

PEANUT BUTTER

I was probably eleven or twelve the first time I ever tasted peanut butter. I thought it was the greatest thing God ever made.

One day at school, little Fred Tackett had peanut butter and jam between two pieces of light bread. I had never seen light bread before, so I traded a biscuit and blackberry jam for half of his sandwich. And, man, that was the greatest thing I ever tasted.

He threw the other half of the sandwich in the creek. I went down the creek trying to catch it because I was going to eat it. But when it passed me, it was just in little flakes. And I cried. I cried because that was something we never had.

I still love peanut butter. I like to put peanut butter in candy and cakes and stuff that I make. My kids don't think it's special, but I do. I imagine it's from the time when I was a kid.

Loretta in the cowgirl outfit she made in the 1960s.

BUTTERMILK PIE

MAKES 8 SERVINGS

The easiest way to test if your pies and cakes are done is to take a clean butter knife and insert it into the center of your baked pie or cake. If the knife comes out clean, it's done.

$1\frac{1}{2}$	CUPS SUGAR
$\frac{1}{4}$	CUP BUTTER, SOFTENED
3	EGGS, SLIGHTLY BEATEN
4	TABLESPOONS ALL-PURPOSE FLOUR
	DASH OF SALT
$1\frac{1}{4}$	CUPS BUTTERMILK
$\frac{1}{4}$	TEASPOON GROUND NUTMEG
1	TEASPOON VANILLA EXTRACT
1	UNBAKED (9-INCH) PIE SHELL

Preheat the oven to 350°. In a large bowl combine the sugar and butter and beat until creamy. Add the eggs, flour, and salt and beat until light and fluffy. Fold in the buttermilk, nutmeg, and vanilla. Pour the mixture into the pie shell. Bake for 45 to 50 minutes. Cool before cutting.

FUDGE PIE

MAKES 12 SERVINGS

4	(1-OUNCE) SQUARES UNSWEETENED BAKING CHOCOLATE
2	STICKS BUTTER
$2\frac{2}{3}$	CUPS SUGAR
$\frac{2}{3}$	CUP ALL-PURPOSE FLOUR
4	EGGS
2	TEASPOONS VANILLA EXTRACT
2	UNBAKED (9-INCH) PIE SHELLS

Preheat the oven to 350°. In a saucepan melt the chocolate and butter over low heat, stirring constantly. Stir in the sugar and cook until dissolved. Add the flour, eggs, and vanilla and stir until smooth. Pour the mixture into the pie shells and bake for 30 minutes. Cool before cutting.

OLD-FASHIONED MOLASSES PIE

MAKES 8 SERVINGS

1	CUP MOLASSES
3	EGGS
½	CUP BUTTER, SOFTENED
1	TEASPOON VANILLA EXTRACT
1	CUP SUGAR
1	(9-INCH) PIE SHELL

Preheat the oven to 350°. Whip the molasses in a medium bowl until light. In a separate bowl, mix the eggs, butter, vanilla, and sugar. Add the egg mixture to the whipped molasses. Pour into the pie shell. Bake for 15 minutes. Reduce the oven to 150° and continue to bake for 10 minutes or until the pie is set. Cool before cutting.

Patsy and Peggy in the 1960s.

LORETTA'S FAVORITE CHOCOLATE PIE

MAKES 12 SERVINGS

PIE

2	CUPS SUGAR
5	TABLESPOONS CORNSTARCH
2	CUPS MILK
3	TABLESPOONS BUTTER
$\frac{1}{2}$	CUP COCOA
	DASH OF SALT
2	BAKED (8-INCH) PIE SHELLS

TOPPING

5	EGG WHITES
$\frac{1}{8}$	TEASPOON CREAM OF TARTAR
$\frac{1}{3}$	CUP CONFECTIONERS' SUGAR
1	TABLESPOON VANILLA EXTRACT

For the pie, in a medium saucepan mix together the sugar and cornstarch. Add the milk, butter, cocoa, and salt. Cook over medium heat. Divide the mixture between the pie shells. Preheat the oven to 350°.

For the topping, in a mixing bowl beat the egg whites, cream of tartar, and sugar together with a hand mixer until light and stiff. Stir in the vanilla. Spread the topping over each pie. Bake until the tops are lightly brown, about 8 minutes. Cool before cutting.

CHOCOLATE PIE

The first time I met Doo was at a pie social at the schoolhouse in Butcher Holler. We didn't have windows in the schoolroom. The ornery kids had broken out about eight or nine of them in the summertime. When wintertime came, we were freezing to death. We were around a big ol' round coal stove that sat right in the middle of the schoolroom.

I came up with the idea for the pie social. I told the teacher, "Let's have a pie supper and get enough money to put the windows back in the school room, and it won't be so cold." She said that'd be fine but that I'd have to handle it. I told her I would. I went up and down Butcher Holler, hollering, "There's a pie supper at the schoolhouse!" I'd make somebody come out on the porch if I hollered loud enough, but I didn't go in.

We had the pie supper on the 10th day of December. Everybody brought pies. Before it started, we were all outside with our coats on, playing Ring Around the Roses and all them little school games. Kids could stick their heads in a tub of water and try to get an apple out. There was all kinds of games. We were playing a game where whoever got in the middle of the ring had to kiss the boy. You can bet I was trying not to get in the middle of the ring. But I did, and Doo kissed me. Then he put my hands in his great big old Army coat. It was cold, and he took my hand in his and put it in the pocket of his jacket. Well, I knew that was a little funny, but I didn't know why.

Doolittle bid the pies off that night. The teacher had talked to Doo's mother and said, "We don't have nobody to bid the pies off." His mother said, "I'll talk to Doo. He may come out and do it." And he did. But he scooted my pie back. I thought, "What's wrong with my pie?" I wondered why he wouldn't let nobody buy my pie.

Any boy who bought a pie from a girl who was old enough got to walk the girl home. Well, that wasn't even in my mind. I wasn't old enough, I didn't think. But Doolittle bought my pie for five dollars. It was a chocolate pie, but instead of using sugar in it, I used salt.

Mommy had the salt and sugar in little brown paper sacks. We called 'em brown paper pokes. Mommy had the sugar and the salt in the same size sacks, so I used the salt instead of the sugar. Oh, I was smart. I thought, "Oh, boy, this pie turned out great," not knowin' my mix-up.

Well, Doo took a big bite of the pie, and he went straight outside. His reaction was just like in the movie. I didn't know what was wrong with him. I thought maybe there was something wrong, he was going to the toilet or something. I thought, "He don't like my cookin'." When he come back into the schoolhouse, he says, "Loretta, have you tasted of the pie?" I said, "No, I was waiting for you." He said, "Honey, I think you made this with salt, not sugar." I said, "No! I put sugar in it!" I tasted of it, and I could not believe what I'd done. It was a salt pie, no kidding.

He had gone out to spit it out. I couldn't believe that, but that was my first cooking. After that, if Mommy let me make anything, like cookies or anything, I would always taste of the salt and the sugar and bring out the sugar, not the salt.

Doo took me home that night. He wanted to drive me in his Jeep, but I wouldn't get in it. It scared me to death. It looked like it was from outer space. I said, "I'm not getting in that thing!" He said, "I can take you all the way to the house." I said, "I'm not getting in it."

Daddy had made pine torches for us to walk with. So I made him walk me home then go all the way back to the schoolhouse with a pine torch and take his Jeep home because I wouldn't get in it.

Daddy's sisters and all my cousins were at our house, and I walked in the house a-humming. Mommy said, "Loretty, who brought you home tonight?" Just real snappy, I said, "Doolittle Lynn." She said, "Don't you ever let me hear of you being with him again. He's too old for you."

About two nights later, here comes Doolittle. I heard this awful sound and thought, "What's going on?" So I run out on the porch, and here comes Doo in that doggone Jeep, up the holler and right into the yard. Scared me to death. And I knew Daddy was going to kill him. Doo come up and said, "I'm here to see Loretty." He started calling me "Loretty," and from then on we took his Jeep. One month to the day after that pie supper, Doo and I got married.

179

SOUTHERN SOFT CUSTARD

MAKES 4 SERVINGS

1	EGG
2	EGG YOLKS
$\frac{1}{4}$	CUP SUGAR
$\frac{1}{8}$	TEASPOON SALT
1	TEASPOON VANILLA EXTRACT
$1\frac{1}{2}$	CUPS MILK
1	TABLESPOON COLORED SUGAR FOR GARNISH
1	TABLESPOON GROUND NUTMEG FOR GARNISH

Slightly beat the egg and egg yolks. Combine the eggs, sugar, salt, and vanilla in a saucepan. Add the milk and blend well. Cook over medium heat until the mixture thinly coats a spoon, stirring constantly. Remove from the heat and beat vigorously. Pour into serving dishes and cool. Use as a sauce for fruit, cake, or other desserts. Garnish with colored sugar or nutmeg.

OLD-FASHIONED BREAD PUDDING

MAKES 6 TO 8 SERVINGS

This is an easy and great way to use up your week-old stale bread.

2	EGGS
$1\frac{1}{2}$	TEASPOONS GROUND CINNAMON
1	(5-OUNCE) CAN EVAPORATED MILK
1	TEASPOON VANILLA EXTRACT
$\frac{1}{2}$	CUP SUGAR
3	CUPS BREADCRUMBS
$\frac{1}{2}$	CUP RAISINS
$\frac{1}{2}$	CUP OF YOUR FAVORITE CHOPPED NUTS (I LIKE WALNUTS)

Preheat the oven to 350°. In a large bowl combine the eggs, cinnamon, evaporated milk, vanilla, and sugar and mix well. Add the breadcrumbs, raisins, and nuts, stirring well. Spread the mixture in a well-greased 9-inch baking dish. Bake until the top is golden brown, about 10 minutes.

DECORATION DAY

On the 30th of May we always decorated graves. We'd all fix something to put on the graves. Mommy would fix flowers out of crepe paper. She'd make the leaves, the stems, and everything. The next day, we'd take them back on the hill, which was a mile straight up, to decorate the graves.

We'd have a little meeting in the schoolhouse. I'd stand by the door in the schoolhouse because I just knew that schoolhouse could fall any time. The preacher, he was a first cousin of Daddy's. He would get going, thumping and a-carryin' on. He cupped his ear with his hand while he was a-preachin', and he didn't give up. When he started, friends, forget it. I knew the schoolhouse would fall, so I'd stand by the door. That way, if it started to fall, I could run out.

Daddy's sister and all them, they'd either cook and we'd go to their place, or Mommy would cook and they'd come to our place. It's not like today, people all getting together and cooking. That didn't happen. So Decoration Day was the biggest day in our life except for Christmas. Of course, Mommy would try to kill a chicken. She didn't kill many chickens, because she had them for eggs . . . what would lay.

And we always had banana pudding. Oh, that was the greatest thing that ever happened to us, banana pudding. I looked forward to Decoration Day all year long because I knew it meant we'd get banana pudding. That was a great treat for us, and to this day there's not much I like more than a good banana pudding.

Loretta's mom, Clara Webb, in the early 1970s.

182

BANANA PUDDING

MAKES 16 SERVINGS

2	EGGS, SEPARATED
1	CUP MILK
$\frac{3}{4}$	CUP PLUS 1 TABLESPOON SUGAR
2	TABLESPOONS FLOUR
	PINCH OF SALT
1	TEASPOON VANILLA EXTRACT
1	(12-OUNCE) BOX VANILLA WAFERS
8	LARGE RIPE BANANAS, SLICED

Preheat the oven to 350°. In the top of a double boiler combine the egg yolks and milk. Mix in ¾ cup of the sugar, the flour, and salt. Cook over simmering water, stirring constantly, until thick. Remove from the heat and add the vanilla.

In a 13 x 9-inch baking dish, alternate layers of vanilla wafers and bananas, spreading the pudding between each layer, ending with the pudding. Beat the egg whites in a mixing bowl with an electric mixer until foamy. Slowly add the remaining 1 tablespoon sugar, beating at high speed until slightly stiff and shiny. Spread the meringue over the pudding and cook in the oven until brown, about 8 minutes.

CHOCOLATE & MARSHMALLOW CAKE

MAKES 12 SERVINGS

2	STICKS BUTTER, MELTED
2	CUPS SUGAR
4	EGGS
1	TEASPOON VANILLA EXTRACT
$\frac{1}{2}$	CUP COCOA POWDER
$1\frac{1}{4}$	CUPS ALL-PURPOSE FLOUR
1	TEASPOON SALT
1	(10-OUNCE) BAG MINIATURE MARSHMALLOWS

Preheat the oven to 350°. In a large bowl beat the butter, sugar, eggs, and vanilla until blended. Beat in the cocoa powder, flour, and salt. Pour the mixture into a buttered 13 x 9-inch baking pan and bake for 20 to 25 minutes. Remove the cake from the oven and spread the marshmallows evenly over the top. Turn off the oven and return the cake to the oven to melt the marshmallows.

CHOCOLATE & MARSHMALLOW CAKE ICING

MAKES ENOUGH FOR 2 CAKES

$1\frac{1}{2}$	(16-OUNCE) BOXES CONFECTIONERS' SUGAR
1	STICK BUTTER, MELTED
$\frac{1}{2}$	CUP COCOA
1	TEASPOON VANILLA EXTRACT
	HALF-AND-HALF

In a large mixing bowl beat the confectioners' sugar, butter, cocoa, and vanilla together. Beating continuously, gradually add a little at a time enough half-and-half to make the icing smooth and creamy. Swirl the icing over the cake after the marshmallows have melted but are still hot.

GOOEY CAKE

MAKES 12 SERVINGS

1	BOX GERMAN CHOCOLATE CAKE MIX
1	(14-OUNCE) CAN SWEETENED CONDENSED MILK
1	JAR CARAMEL TOPPING
1	CUP WHIPPED TOPPING (COOL WHIP)
3	FROZEN ENGLISH TOFFEE HEATH BARS, CRUSHED

Prepare and bake the cake according to the package directions, using a 13 x 9-inch cake pan. While warm, poke holes with a straw halfway into the cake about 1 inch apart. Drizzle the condensed milk into the holes. Pour the caramel topping over the cake and refrigerate for 1 hour. When cool, spread the whipped topping on the cake and sprinkle the crushed toffee bars over the top. Refrigerate overnight before serving.

ANGEL FOOD CAKE

Grandma Lynn could make the best angel food cakes, and every birthday she'd give me one. I loved those angel food cakes because she used egg-white icing. I don't care for the icing that's made out of confectioners' sugar and shortening. Doo's mother would put that egg-white icing about an inch tall all the way around it, and it wasn't too sweet. She made me one of those cakes for my birthday three or four times before Doo and I moved to Washington. I had to learn how to do everything for myself then, and I learned how to do that, too.

HOMEMADE PEACH CAKE

MAKES 12 SERVINGS

CAKE

1	(29-OUNCE) CAN SLICED PEACHES
2	EGGS
2	CUPS SELF-RISING FLOUR
1	TEASPOON GROUND CINNAMON
1	TEASPOON BAKING SODA
½	(29-OUNCE) CAN PEACH SYRUP (THE SYRUP THAT THE PEACHES CAME IN)
1	STICK BUTTER, SOFTENED

FROSTING

1	CUP SUGAR
¾	CUP EVAPORATED MILK
1	STICK BUTTER, SOFTENED

For the cake, preheat the oven to 350°. Drain the peaches, reserving half the syrup. Chop the peaches. In a medium mixing bowl beat the eggs until light. Add the flour, cinnamon, baking soda, peaches, reserved peach syrup, and butter and beat until well blended. Pour the batter into a well-greased 13 x 9-inch baking pan. Bake for 35 to 40 minutes.

For the frosting, in a mixing bowl combine the sugar, evaporated milk, and butter. Mix until smooth and the frosting coats a spoon. It takes about 5 minutes of stirring. Spread the frosting over the warm cake.

LEMON WHIPPERSNAPPERS

MAKES 24 SERVINGS

1	(18½-OUNCE) PACKAGE LEMON CAKE MIX
1	LARGE EGG, BEATEN
2¼	CUPS WHIPPED TOPPING (COOL WHIP), THAWED
	SIFTED POWDERED SUGAR

Preheat the oven to 350°. In a large bowl combine the cake mix, egg, and Cool Whip and mix until blended. Sift the powdered sugar onto the wax paper. Drop a teaspoon of the mixture into the sugar and roll to coat. Place on a cookie sheet and bake for 10 to 15 minutes or until lightly brown.

Peggy and Patsy Lynn in 1973.

STRAWBERRY & RHUBARB PIE

MAKES 8 SLICES

3	CUPS CHOPPED RHUBARB, ABOUT $\frac{1}{4}$ TO $\frac{1}{2}$ INCH THICK
1	CUP SLICED FRESH STRAWBERRIES
$1\frac{1}{2}$	CUPS SUGAR
3	TABLESPOONS QUICK-COOKING TAPIOCA
$\frac{1}{2}$	TEASPOON NUTMEG
$\frac{1}{4}$	TEASPOON SALT
1	(9-INCH) PIE SHELL
	BUTTER

Preheat the oven to 400°. Mix the rhubarb, strawberries, sugar, tapioca, nutmeg, and salt in a large bowl. Set aside for 20 to 30 minutes. Stir occasionally. Pour the fruit mixture into the pie shell and dot with butter. Bake for 40 minutes.

STRAWBERRIES

I got strawberries every summer while we lived in Washington. After the strawberry picking was over, they'd let me go back into the fields. They'd let me get all I could pick, just like Ruth gleaning the fields in the Bible. I would pick strawberries and put 'em up and freeze 'em.

I picked raspberries the same way. I climbed them trees and picked raspberries. Just about all the fruit that we had, that's the way I did it. I'd freeze it or can it. Them people in Washington state was good to me. I had four kids while we were out there, and the folks in Washington was looking out for me a little bit.

APPLE TURNOVERS

MAKES 12 SERVINGS

3	CUPS ALL-PURPOSE FLOUR
2	TABLESPOONS GRANULATED SUGAR
$1\frac{1}{2}$	TEASPOONS SALT
$\frac{1}{2}$	TEASPOON GROUND CINNAMON
$1\frac{1}{4}$	CUPS SHORTENING
5 to 6	TABLESPOONS WATER
1	(20- TO 22-OUNCE) CAN PREPARED APPLE PIE FILLING
	CONFECTIONERS' SUGAR

Preheat the oven to 425°. In a large bowl combine the flour, granulated sugar, salt, and cinnamon. Cut in the shortening. Add the water 1 tablespoon at a time, mixing with a fork until the mixture forms a ball. On a lightly floured surface, roll half the dough into a 10 x 15-inch rectangle. Cut into 5-inch squares. Repeat with the other half of the dough. Spoon about 2 tablespoons of the fruit filling onto each square. Fold each square over to form a triangle. Seal the edge by pressing firmly with a fork. Pierce the top of each triangle with a fork. Bake on ungreased baking sheets for 12 to 15 minutes. Cool slightly. Sprinkle with confectioners' sugar.

FROSTED PECANS

MAKES 1 POUND PECANS

1	POUND PECAN HALVES
2	EGG WHITES
1	CUP SUGAR
1	TABLESPOON HONEY
1	STICK MARGARINE

Heat oven to 250°. Spread the pecans in a single layer on a large baking sheet and bake for 10 to 15 minutes. Remove from the oven. Increase the temperature to 325°. In a large bowl beat the egg whites, sugar, and honey until creamy. Add the pecans to the bowl and stir until well coated. Melt the margarine in a large cake pan. Spread the pecans in a single layer into the pan. Bake for 30 minutes, stirring every 10 minutes.

FUDGE CANDY

MAKES 16 SQUARES

2	CUPS SUGAR
$\frac{1}{3}$	CUP COCOA
$\frac{2}{3}$	CUP HEAVY CREAM
$\frac{1}{2}$	TEASPOON SALT
$\frac{1}{2}$	STICK BUTTER
1	TEASPOON VANILLA EXTRACT

In a heavy saucepan combine the sugar, cocoa, cream, and salt. Cook slowly over medium heat to the soft-ball stage on a candy thermometer or until a small amount of the mixture dropped in cold water forms a soft ball. Remove from the heat and stir in the butter and vanilla. Pour into a greased 8 x 8-inch baking dish. Cut into squares after cooling.

ICE CREAM

The first time I ever tasted ice cream it came from John L. Lewis. I'll never forget him. John L. Lewis took over the coal mine unions. He ran the United Mine Workers of America for forty years. Daddy put his picture up in our dining room. He had great big fuzzy eyebrows. I'll never forget those.

When Daddy come home one Christmas, John L. Lewis had given every worker a gallon of ice cream. That was not long before I got married. That was the first time I ever eat ice cream. We just didn't have ice cream.

Patsy Cline and I would make ice cream when we'd get together. A lot of times I made it when I come home. But I don't really have the time now, and the kids are not here. Kids are really ruined today, anyway. All the grandkids get all the ice cream they want.

FRUIT ICE

MAKES 6 TO 8 SERVINGS

	JUICE OF 3 ORANGES
	JUICE OF 3 LEMONS
3	BANANAS, MASHED
3	CUPS SUGAR
2	CUPS WATER
3	EGG WHITES

Mix the orange juice, lemon juice, bananas, sugar, and water in a bowl. Beat the egg whites until stiff and fold them into the banana mixture. Freeze overnight.

SNOW CREAM

Snow cream, I guess, was the closest to ice cream as you could get. When it snowed, Mommy would take a dishpan and clean it real good. Then she would go out and take the snow from the top of the porch. It was low, and she could stand up in a chair and reach up there and take the layer off the top. She would get that dishpan at least two-thirds full of snow so she could mix everything else up with it.

Mommy would break three eggs, beat 'em up real good, and pour them into the snow. She would take about a spoonful of vanilla flavoring, and she'd pour it in there. Then she just kept putting sugar in until she got it sweet enough. She'd put in a half cup of sugar, and then she'd taste it. Then she'd put another half cup and taste it to see if it was sweet enough.

There was eight kids and her and Daddy, so there'd have to be a lot of snow to make snow cream. But in Kentucky, where we lived, when it started snowing it might snow ten inches or so. I'd always hope there'd be enough for snow cream. And usually there was. We just went crazy for it.

Loretta's mother, Clara, Patsy, Peggy, and Loretta in 1968.

★ INDEX ★

INDEX

INDEX

INDEX

INDEX

INDEX

INDEX

INDEX

INDEX